T5-CWL-422

THE POETICS OF SPEECH IN THE MEDIEVAL SPANISH EPIC

MATTHEW BAILEY

The Poetics of Speech
in the Medieval Spanish Epic

UNIVERSITY OF TORONTO PRESS
Toronto Buffalo London

© University of Toronto Press Incorporated 2010
Toronto Buffalo London
www.utppublishing.com
Printed in Canada

ISBN 978-1-4426-4156-3

Printed on acid-free, 100% post-consumer recycled paper with
vegetable-based inks.

Library and Archives Canada Cataloguing in Publication

Bailey, Matthew
    The poetics of speech in the medieval Spanish epic / Matthew Bailey.

    Includes bibliographical references and index.
    ISBN 978-1-4426-4156-3

    1. Epic poetry, Spanish – History and criticism. 2. Spanish poetry – To 1500
    – History and criticism. I. Title.

    PQ6088.B34 2010   861'.0320901   C2010-900656-9

University of Toronto Press acknowledges the financial assistance to its
publishing program of the Canada Council for the Arts and the Ontario Arts
Council.

  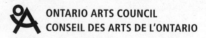

University of Toronto Press acknowledges the financial support for its publishing activities of the Government of Canada through the Book Publishing
Industry Development Program (BPIDP).

In memory of Paul Bailey and Margaret Beale-Bailey

Contents

Acknowledgments

This book was conceived in the passing of the *Pear Stories* from a shelf in the faculty office of Thomas Montgomery at Tulane University into my hands, with the simple directive: 'You may be able to make some use of this.' From this brief exchange in 1984 to the publication of the present volume, a career has taken shape, accompanied and assisted by many good people – in the early years by Tom Montgomery, but also by Samuel Armistead and Alan Deyermond, giants of the field who inspired and deigned to mentor a multitude of aspiring scholars. More recently I have been sustained by my peers, perhaps the most prominent among them Mercedes Vaquero and Irene Zaderenko, active scholars who take the time to engage and to energize their colleagues and students alike. I would like to thank generous colleagues at the institutions where I have worked, the College of the Holy Cross, the University of Texas at Austin, and now Washington and Lee University, and their programs for research leave. Most of all, thank you to my loving family, patient and understanding always.

THE POETICS OF SPEECH IN THE MEDIEVAL SPANISH EPIC

Introduction

There is abundant evidence of a vibrant tradition of epic poetry disseminated orally in Spain during the Middle Ages. Perhaps the best example of its prominence can be found in the many heroic narratives that were incorporated as prose text into the *Estoria de España*, the first vernacular history of Spain sponsored and guided by Alfonso X, king of León-Castile (1252–84).[1] The learned chroniclers of this royal enterprise based their historical narrative on two thirteenth-century histories originally written in Latin.[2] But they were also obliged to include the more compelling oral narratives circulating at the time, which focused primarily on the Castilian warrior elite.[3] When these oral versions of events contradicted the written Latin sources, the learned chroniclers naturally favoured the written versions. They made their bias and their ambivalence clear in the text by casting doubt on the reliability of the oral sources, but then transcribing them in their entirety anyway.[4] The Latin sources, despite the stature and authority of their authors, were no match for the evocative power of the epic, honed through the dynamic interplay of poet and audience over generations.[5]

The protagonists of these heroic tales were not the kings chronicled in the Latin texts, but warriors from the Castilian nobility who had fallen into disfavour or challenged the authority of their lord or king. Fernán González, Gonzalo González, and Bernardo del Carpio are a few of the uncompromising nobles whose deeds enliven the latter portion of Alfonso's history of Spain (Vaquero 1994). Unfortunately for us today, most of these tales were never preserved in verse or, if they were put to parchment, were subsequently lost. The epic narratives that do survive in verse are the *Cantar de Mio Cid* and the *Mocedades de Rodrigo*, both of which recreate in legendary fashion the warrior deeds of Rodrigo

Díaz de Vivar, better known as El Cid, and the *Poema de Fernán González*. The *Fernán González* is generally not considered a true epic due to its considerable clerical influence, most notable in its learned compositional style known as *cuaderna vía*. Yet its protagonist, count Fernán González of Castile, is most certainly cut from the same heroic cloth as the legendary Cid.

The *Cid* is the best known of the three extant Spanish epic poems. Its date of placement onto parchment is given as 1207 in the closing lines of the text. The poem narrates episodes from the later years of the life of Rodrigo Díaz de Vivar, focusing on his exile by king Alfonso VI and his subsequent struggle to return to royal favour. His return to the king's good graces occurs after the conquest of the Moorish kingdom of Valencia, which actually took place in 1094 and is certainly a deed worthy of lasting fame. But the narration of the Valencia conquest is complete by line 1220, and yet the poem continues for another 2515 lines, narrating fanciful episodes with little or no relationship to historical fact. The *Mocedades*, so named because it recreates the deeds of the young Rodrigo Díaz, is more extravagant than the *Cid* in that virtually none of the hero's actions can be documented historically.[6] The date of the *Mocedades* manuscript is given as 1400, although the text is most certainly copied from an earlier version. A similar narrative of Rodrigo's youth was incorporated into the first post-Alfonsine prose history of Castile, known as the *Crónica de Castilla* (ca 1295), but its portrayal of the Castilian king Fernando I is sufficiently distinct from that of the *Mocedades* as to render it of limited use in dating the poem. The most likely date for the poem relates its unique portrayal of king Fernando I to the worrisome minority of the Castilian king Fernando IV (1295–1312), and so assumes a composition soon after his death (Bailey 2007, 6–7). The manuscript version of the *Fernán González* is thought to date from 1250, some three hundred years after the most active period in the life of the Castilian count it portrays. It is highly unlikely that any of the events recreated in the poem are anything more than dim memories of historical events, although sparse documentation makes even that meagre claim of historical accuracy difficult to prove. The historical documentation of his tenth-century exploits suggests that Fernán González was a fairly successful warrior who managed to maintain his considerable stature through a combination of fierce resistance to Christian and Muslim enemies and alliances through marriage.[7] In his legendary life he is portrayed in a similar way, but with a stronger emphasis on his success in battle, and especially as a rebel Castilian warrior who achieves the independence of Castile from León through his willingness to fight Christians and Moors alike when others, including the upper nobility and kings, are desperate to avoid armed conflict with the Moor.

It seems reasonable to assume that the Fernán González narrative would have appealed to the same audiences as the Cid poems. The clerical style and expression of the poem exemplify the efforts of the learned men of the Church to create a rival vernacular narrative poetry for their own purposes, in this case to preach a gospel of consecration for warrior deeds. Neither this poem nor the other narratives of the medieval warrior class of Castile are powered by historical fact, but by the collective genius of a poetic tradition that is unique to its historical and social context. These narratives moved audiences throughout the Middle Ages and subsequently inspired innumerable folk ballads and a number of dramatic works by prominent Renaissance authors such as Guillén de Castro and Lope de Vega. Beyond the borders of Spain the French playwright Pierre Corneille, the English Romantic Robert Southey, and more recently the Hollywood movie magnate Samuel Bronston have all felt compelled to recreate episodes from the life of Rodrigo Díaz. The *Cid* continues to appeal to readers today, while other Spanish medieval texts are studied only by specialists, because they seem either quaint or ponderous and impenetrable. The universal nature of this appeal has not been identified, nor for the most part has it been an object of study.

The *Cid* is uniquely evocative among medieval Spanish literary texts, without equal until the fourteenth-century *Libro de buen amor*. It shares many expressive characteristics with other oral narrative traditions, but learned influences have also been identified. Among Hispano-medievalists, specialists in the medieval literature of Spain, it is generally assumed that oral composition and writing were mutually exclusive endeavours, representative of two distinct worlds, the unlettered and the learned; the learned influences in the *Cid* have led specialists to conclude that Spanish epic poems were composed in writing. The expressive features identified as related to oral poetry are considered remnants from narratives that a learned author assimilated and reproduced as part of a written composition. But the issue is open to question since the compositional model that Hispano-medievalists have devised for the Spanish epic is not the same as the model of medieval composition that has emerged in related fields of study. Historians in general as well as linguists assume that the European Middle Ages were essentially oral, in that writing was dictated and reading was done 'viva

voce' (Fleischmann 1990a, 20). In fact, the most distinguishing characteristic of this period may well be its unique mix of orality and writing,
a circumstance akin to Zumthor's notion of 'mixed orality where the
influence of the written remains external to it, as well as partial or re-
tarded' (Zumthor 1990, 25).

An awareness of the mixed orality of medieval literature and of the
oral nature of much of the expression in the *Cid* has led scholars to affirm that the poet of the *Cid* either recited his poem after composing it
and retaining it in his memory, or composed it first in writing and then
recited it. Accompanying this concept of a text composed in memory or
in writing is the fairly vehement rejection of an improvised oral performance of the poem, in the manner of the Serbo-Croatian *guslari*, and
the simultaneous transcription of the poem onto parchment as an orally
dictated text (Montaner 2007, 94–5).[8] Yet the documented evidence of
how texts were composed in the thirteenth century does not lend cre-
dence to the idea of vernacular texts being composed in memory or in
writing. There are, however, many examples of oral composition by
learned men, and these examples make abundantly clear that the process involved the oral dictation by the author to a scribe or scribes for
initial transcription onto wax tablets, followed by a process of editing
before making a fair copy on parchment.[9]

The narrative poems of this study, the *Cid*, the *Mocedades*, and the
Fernán González, are vernacular works, composed by minstrels, and so
very different from the compositions composed in Latin by the learned
clerics studied by historians. Yet the decision to put these narratives to
parchment was inevitably made by a cleric in a position of authority.
The process of writing them down, first onto wax tablets and subsequently onto parchment, would have been supervised by clerics and
carried out by the same class of scribes described by Clanchy (1979,
216–18) and Carruthers (1990, 6). Previous studies have identified various degrees of learned influence in these poems, whether in the subject
matter, the verse form, or the expression. This learned influence is sufficient to assume some degree of clerical intervention in the process of
transforming these oral narratives into three manuscript texts. Yet the
texts also retain varying degrees of oral expression, something no
longer present in the learned prose texts preserved in Latin.

Prose compositions have no metrical strictures, and we may assume
that the scribes who put them into writing had the ability to restructure
them after their initial oral delivery by the author. Verse, on the other
hand, whether it be the assonance-based verse of the *Cid* and the

Mocedades, or the syllable-count verse with end-rhyme of the *cuaderna vía* poem *Fernán González*, links expression and meaning intimately. Verses may be added, or even deleted, but reworking the original verses would require a significant poetic sensibility on the part of the scribes, a skill they could not be expected to have as professional transcribers, not composers. What the epic text preserved on parchment affords us is a close approximation to the original dictation from minstrel to scribe, to the unfiltered language of thirteenth-century Castile, and, most importantly, to what an audience of the time would have heard in performance.

The most compelling aspect of the Spanish epic may well be its expression and the degree to which that expression retains the flavour of the original dictated work. The objective of this study is to examine these Spanish epic texts, and to determine the extent to which their unique expression is linked to their original oral delivery. This task will be initially supported by the findings of Wallace Chafe, a linguist who has analysed contemporary speech and has been able to distinguish some characteristics of spoken versus written language. Chafe has linked the peculiar characteristics of spoken discourse to the cognitive processes deployed in the production of what he initially terms spontaneous speech. He finds that the essential component of cognitively based speech is the intonation unit, which corresponds in an uncanny way to the epic hemistich, or half-line, which is the basic unit of expression of the Spanish epic (Bailey 2003, 262). A similar finding in Homeric poetry by Egbert Bakker is especially encouraging, given the fact that the Homeric poems have a more intimate relationship with the written medium than do the Spanish epic poems. Finally, the analysis of the expression of these poems should lead to a more thorough understanding of their compositional process, all of which will help us to hear the poems in a more genuine and culturally attuned way.

Before we venture into an analysis of the poems, a review of the history of the relevant scholarship on their composition will help us understand how we arrived at the present state of affairs. This will be the task of the next chapter.

1 The Critical Response to Oral Composition

The extent to which oral expression shapes the Spanish epic has been a lively issue among Hispano-medievalists, although the polemical question of its oral composition has been effectively shelved in favour of an approach that allows for varying degrees of literate and oral influences.[1] The modern understanding of the Spanish epic begins with the work of Ramón Menéndez Pidal, who published extensively throughout the first half of the twentieth century. The exceptional quality of his work is manifested by its continued relevance among scholars, and by the fact that many of the current assumptions about the *Cid* can be traced directly to him. For Menéndez Pidal epic poetry is inspired in the emotional and poetic narration of contemporary events (1963, 189). It is written poetry, composed in a style appropriate for oral performance before expectant audiences (200–2).[2] The metrical style is kept simple as an aid to memorization of the poem and to facilitate its reconstruction when memory fails during performance (203). In the ballad tradition that he understood as emerging nearly simultaneously with the disappearance of the epic, Menéndez Pidal distinguished two forms of transmission, one oral and the other written, although he saw both as originating in writing. In his view, the folk ballads (*romances tradicionales*) were originally based on episodes from the medieval epic but were transformed aesthetically as they passed orally from one generation to another among the uncultured populace 'de gente inculta' (1924, 416). The second tradition was of ballads written by professional poets who followed in the tradition of those who had once dedicated themselves to composing the longer epic narratives. He termed these written ballads *romances juglarescos* (minstrel ballads, or ballads of the professional poets), in order to distinguish them from the *romances tradicionales*. By the end of the fifteenth century, ballads were wildly popular among all social classes (1924, 420), but in neither of the two ballad traditions he outlined did Menéndez Pidal imagine a process of oral composition taking place.

It may be worth noting that Menéndez Pidal did not know the work of Milman Parry, probably because Parry's work was directed to Homeric scholars. Parry had envisioned comparing his initial findings from Homeric poetry and his subsequent observations of South Slavic poetry with the medieval European epics (Adam Parry 1971, 377, 392–3; Lord 1948, 37), but his untimely death prevented him from completing this project. Both Parry and Menéndez Pidal recognized the use of formulas as an element of the poetics of epic expression, although Menéndez Pidal understood them as either expressions common to all (*tópicos vulgares*), or as unique expressions attributable to a particular poet (*tópicos literarios*), and not in relation to epic metre, syntax or, therefore, as an indicator of oral composition (1963, 97–105, 201–2). Parry's first two publications, theses that he published in 1928 as part of his doctoral program at the University of Paris, focused on the abundant noun-epithet formulas in Homer. He explained them as part of a poetic grammar related to the structure of the verse, traditional and independent of a poet's free will (Parry, 1971, esp. 21–3, 189–90).[3] His conclusion, stated briefly at the outset of his thesis, was that 'the use of the fixed epithet … is entirely dependent on its convenience in versification' (1971, 22), thus emphasizing the irrelevance of a modern aesthetic appreciation for the fixed epithet as something associated with the poet's artistry. But Parry soon came to view what he termed the Homeric style, meaning the peculiar abundance of ready-made formulaic expressions developed over generations of poets, as a response to the demands of a metrically complex verse form composed orally in performance. By the time he had returned to the United States and published his first article in English (Parry 1930), Parry had confirmed that what he had initially understood as traditionality, the abundance of expressions that were used repeatedly to comply with a specific metrical requirement, was in reality a consequence or function of the constraints on the poet who composed orally before an expectant audience (Parry 1971, esp. 269–70, 322–4).

Parry's work had found no echo in the study of Spanish epic poetry until Albert B. Lord published *The Singer of Tales* in 1960, some twenty-five years after Parry's death. Lord had served Parry as a graduate assistant, accompanying him in his fieldwork recording the oral epics of the Yugoslav *guslari*. Lord eventually completed the program of field-work Parry had laid out and published their findings with the more comparative focus that Parry had suggested. Lord had crossed over into the medievalist camp by including a short chapter entitled 'Some Notes on Medieval Epic' in which he applied the findings from his study of the Homeric and Yugoslav poetry to elucidate the oral charac-teristics of the *Chanson de Roland*, *Beowulf*, and a medieval Greek met-rical narrative known as the *Digenis Akritas*. Lord also identified the frequent use of formulas, absence of enjambment, and composition by theme as indicators of oral composition (Lord 1960, 130–1), and medi-evalists soon took note.

In Spanish epic studies the first responses to Lord's work were en-thusiastic, coming from British Hispanists who found in Lord's work an avenue for questioning some of Menéndez Pidal's prevailing as-sumptions about the *Cid*. In the first of these, L.P. Harvey cited Lord's observation that the process of a singer dictating his tale to a scribe can produce metrical irregularities 'that look very much like the Old Spanish *Cid*' (Lord 1960, 127). This led Harvey to suggest that the manuscript text of the *Cid*, with its lack of a discernible metrical scheme, might be a dictated oral text. Lord also documented how in the modern Yugoslav epic tradition every performance of an epic tale deploys trad-itional phrases and themes but never in exactly the same manner, thus producing a unique narrative, specific to that one performance. Lord's observations contrasted sharply with Menéndez Pidal's belief that the divergent Cid narratives found in the Alfonsine chronicles represent written reworkings (*refundiciones*) of the same heroic tale, carried out in response to changes in the attitudes and tastes of their audiences. Thus, Menéndez Pidal's attempt to reconstruct a lost or more perfect *Cid* text from the narratives in the Alfonsine chronicles is termed a 'chimera' by Harvey (1963, 140), and, in another reference to the theories of Menéndez Pidal, 'talk of the first, second, or third versions of the *Cantar de Mio Cid* is nonsense' (142).

A subsequent and ultimately far-reaching response was a brief article by Alan Deyermond, in a kind of prelude to a stellar career that is only now reaching its conclusion.[4] In it Deyermond reviewed some of Lord's essential findings and pointed out their relevance to the two Spanish epic poems. Specifically he noted Lord's findings on the effects of the dictation of oral texts to scribes, as had Harvey, as an explanation for the irregularities in Spanish epic metre, and for the poor structure of the

Mocedades. He continues with the observation that both the *Cid* and the *Mocedades* also show signs of learned influence. These two contrasting observations are resolved in the suggestion that the extant versions of the poems were most likely derived from oral dictation, but that originally they were composed by learned men (Deyermond 1965, 7–8). He ends his article by cautioning that no definitive conclusions regarding the oral or written composition of the poems can be drawn until Lordian tests of formulas, themes, and enjambment are conducted (6 and 8). Although Deyermond acknowledges that Lord's findings include cases of learned men composing orally, he does not specifically suggest this scenario for the Spanish poems.

Deyermond's next publication, now considered a seminal study of the *Mocedades*, promotes a similar scenario, imagining a learned poet with ecclesiastical background writing the text of the *Mocedades* and handing it to *juglares* for oral diffusion, albeit with the following caveat: 'we cannot entirely exclude the idea of a cleric who was also a *juglar* and who could compose orally' (1969, 201n19).[5] Perhaps because he was mindful of the subjective nature of his views on learned authorship, Deyermond regularly expressed a willingness to adjust his conclusions in accordance with future findings, which eventually materialized. Ruth Webber (1980) and Thomas Montgomery (1984a) produced separate responses to Deyermond's scenario of learned authorship and subsequent dictation by a *juglar* to a scribe. These responses led Deyermond to recognize his error and to subsequently exclude oral diffusion of the written text by *juglares*, although he reaffirmed his argument for learned authorship of the *Mocedades* (Deyermond 1999, 14).

Lord's publication came early in the career of Deyermond, but it came very late in the life of Menéndez Pidal, yet his response was vigorous. He focused his attention almost exclusively on Lord's description of the process of oral composition, although he seemed to take little note of the role of formulas and themes in that process. Menéndez Pidal was most concerned by what he termed the singer's improvisation (*improvisación*, or less frequently *repentización*) in recreating an epic tale. The observation by Lord that the best South Slavic singers such as Avdo Mededovic do not recite their poems from memory but instead recreate them from a stock of traditional formulas and themes was ridiculed and deemed irrelevant for comparisons with Homer, the medieval epic, or any other living epic tradition. A single sample should suffice to grasp the tone of Menéndez Pidal's response:

El verdadero poeta, antes de la invención de la escritura, lo mismo que después, aunque se sienta arrebatado por divina inspiración, relexiona, combina, selecciona, depura, corrige y fija en su memoria o en papel lo que después va a producir en público. Lope de Vega, el poeta más espontáneo y fácil de España, decía 'Ríete del poeta que no borra.' En fin, el identificar la creación poética con la improvisación se concibe muy bien entre los poetas como los Yugoslavos, que principalmente actúan ante un proletariado rural; pretender que Homero, cantor ante príncipes y ciudadanos ilustres, tuviese como norma de arte el 'componer *rápidamente* ante un auditorio entusiasta (Lord, p. 149) es, no diré un despropósito literario, por el gran respeto que tengo hacia los dos exploradores que tantas cosas nuevas traen al campo de la investigación, diré sólo que es dejarse llevar demasiado de la afición especialística profesada hacia los cantores yugoslavos, tomándolos como modelo universal de poetas orales. (Menéndez Pidal 1965–6, 200–1)[6]

[The true poet, before the invention of writing, as well as after, even if he feels overcome by divine inspiration, reflects, composes, selects, polishes, corrects, and fixes in his memory or on paper what he will later deliver in public. Lope de Vega, the most spontaneous and natural Spanish poet, said 'Laugh at the poet who does not erase.' In sum, to identify poetic creation with improvisation is understandable among poets like the Yugoslavs, who perform before a rural proletariat; to assume that Homer, singer before princes and illustrious citizens, had as an artistic norm 'rapid composition before a live audience' [quoted here directly from Lord 1960, 149] is, I won't call it a literary absurdity, out of the great respect that I have for these two explorers who have brought so many new things to our field of study, I will say only that to take the Yugoslav singers as a universal model for oral poets is to be overly influenced by the specialistic enthusiasm professed for the Yugoslav singers, taking them as the universal model for oral poets.]

Menéndez Pidal may not have had the energy or the inclination to reconcile the Parry-Lord findings with his belief in written authorship of the Spanish epic. His concept of the oral diffusion of epic and ballad through memorization of a fixed text found little support in Lord's description of the few Yugoslav singers who memorize written narratives, for 'with them the tradition is dead or dying' (Lord 1960, 109). In the final analysis Menéndez Pidal rejected out of hand Lord's model of oral composition for the Spanish epic, noting especially its sparse use of formulas and themes as indicative of an alternate model of composition and transmission, in this case the conservation in memory of the traditional tale. The one exception he noted is the *Mocedades*, in which the poet does innovate out of a desire to completely alter the traditional tale (Menéndez Pidal 1965–6, 210).

Lord's findings did eventually prompt medievalists to re-examine the compositional mode of the Spanish epic. Among the most enthusiastic of these early responders was J.M. Aguirre, who wrote what he termed 'un acercamiento a esta épica con una mente liberada de toda afectación literaria, *strictu sensu*' [an approach to this epic with a mind freed of all literary affectation, strictly speaking] (Aguirre 1968, 13). He cited findings of Lord, as well of C.M. Bowra and K.H. Jackson, and pointed out their relevance to the Spanish epic. Aguirre makes some interesting observations but nothing in the way of concrete findings that future scholars could build upon. This lack of concrete results was soon remedied by a comparatist, Joseph J. Duggan, who quantified the formulaic density of the *Cid* in relation to ten *chansons de geste*, including the *Chanson de Roland*, along with three Old French romances known to have been composed in writing. Duggan found the *Cid* to be 31.7 per cent formulaic, 'slightly more formulaic than the average of ten eleventh and twelfth-century French epics' (30.3 per cent), while the works composed in writing were 16 per cent formulaic. Duggan then established a threshold of 20 per cent formulas or less for works composed in writing, and concluded that the *Cid* 'with 31.7 per cent formulas, is solidly within the range of oral poetry' (Duggan 1974, 268). Equally noteworthy for this study is his affirmation that the *Cid* poet 'did not compose his poem in a way typical of the habits of literate poets' (269). In a later study, Duggan reiterated the relevance of his earlier comparison, specifying that the formulaic density of the *Cid* was 'squarely within the range of the nine *chansons de geste* for which [Jean] Rychner posited oral composition and transmission plus the *Chanson de Roland*' (1989a, 138).

Following Duggan's statistical methodology, John Geary completed a thorough analysis of the formulaic studies on the Spanish epic by identifying and comparing the formulas in the *Cid*, the *Fernán González*, and the *Mocedades*. While Geary found that in the *Cid* formulas account for about a third of its half-lines (31.94 per cent [Geary 1980, 13]), formulaic density in the *Fernán González* (17 per cent) and in the *Mocedades* (14 per cent) is about half that amount (24–5). Geary had assumed that both the *Mocedades* and the *Fernán González* were composed in writing but through his study was able to corroborate Duggan's threshold of no more than 20 per cent formulaic density in written works and to argue for a common formulaic tradition in both written and oral composition (24–5). In spite of the solid methodology employed by Duggan and Geary, Hispano-medievalists have not been inclined to conclude that the *Cid* is orally composed based on formula counts. The current consensus seems to be that the percentage of formulas in the Spanish epic is low in comparison to the percentages of the Homeric poetry studied by Parry (1930, 117–22) and the South Slavic poetry studied by Lord (1960, 45–7), and therefore does not prove oral composition (Deyermond 1987, 43).

The boldest statement for written composition of the *Cid* was made by Colin Smith, who rejected the notion that the extant text had any literary precedent in Spain and accordingly posited a single author, stating that the '*Poema de mio Cid* of 1207 was the first work of its kind in Castilian' (Smith 1983, 23). His claim meant the exclusion from evidence of numerous Latin and vernacular prose chronicles that incorporated tales of warrior deeds depicting seemingly epic events from as far back as the late tenth century. In so doing, Smith dismissed the work of generations of reputable scholars who had come to understand the chronicle narratives as prose versions of orally disseminated epic poems. Smith refers to the arguments for an autochthonous epic tradition pre-dating the *Cid* as nothing more than 'supposition, romantic *espejismo* [delusion], and special pleading' (44). With no literary precedent in Spain, Smith invokes the French epic as the inspiration for his learned poet, making the *Cid* 'a kind of *chanson de geste*, an attempt to emulate and acclimatise the great French genre, but it is also very much more than that, since it is an epic of a new and advanced kind, indeed, a revolutionary interpretation of an established European mode' (73). Based on what he considers his own logical deductions from the evidence of the poem and the period, Smith imagines his poet as 'a literate, well-informed, and cultured man, who composed in writing with a full awareness of the basis of his craft as it had been devised and developed in French' (74). This thirteenth-century Renaissance man was, of all things, a lawyer and none other than the same Per Abbat who identifies himself as the copyist of the poem in its colophon (75).

Most scholars never took the leap of faith Smith asked of them and he eventually disavowed his thinking on the individual authorship of the *Cid*. In an article invoking a reconciliation of ideas about the Spanish epic, Smith characterizes his previous thinking on the Per Abbat authorship of the poem as 'no more than conjectures concerning an act of literary creation in a poorly documented period' (1994, 628). His new scenario for the composition of the *Cid* and other epics does not allow for oral composition either. Smith imagines the poem composed in writing by clerics (*clerici*) utilizing memorized as well as manuscript sources, with a tradition of vernacular verse as a model for their narratives (632). The reconciliation Smith invokes includes his acceptance of a vernacular epic tradition in Spain, initially modelled on the French epic, as argued in a conference paper by Ian Michael, which Smith determined had 'an agreeable logic about it' (623). What Smith does not state explicitly is Michael's recognition of an orally composed, formula-based vernacular epic in Spain that served as the compositional model [*modelo métrico*] for the learned poets who wrote the *Roncesvalles* and the *Cid* in the early thirteenth century (Michael 1992, 82). Michael's thesis, and by extension Smith's, seems similar enough to the ideas of other noted scholars, such as Alan Deyermond (1987, 42–3; 1999, 9–12) and Irene Zaderenko (1998, 88, 126, 153, 170, 188, 191–2), to identify it as one of the principal critical theories regarding the genesis of the extant texts of the Spanish epic.

Smith also identifies an article by Duggan as a step toward reconciliation in that he 'seems to water down the pure milk of Lordian oralist doctrine' (Smith 1994, 626). In truth, Duggan's study describes two ways in which medieval French literature was performed and transmitted, through oral composition and vocal performance. As a comparatist with an extensive knowledge of both French and Spanish medieval literature, Duggan understands oral composition in essentially the same way as Parry and Lord, with a heightened acknowledgment of the role of memory. In the case of the improvisation of a work being performed for the first time, 'memory of the technique of standard phrases and scenes and of performances of other works will come into play' (Duggan 1989b, 49). In the case of the performance of narratives heard or performed before, the poet 'recalls his prior conceptualization of the plot, calls upon models of the type of tale he is telling,' etc. (49). In 'vocal performance,' on the other hand, the purpose is to reproduce from memory a stable text, whether learned from reading a written document, from hearing a written text read aloud, or from another vocal performance (50). No account is given of texts being read from manuscripts.

For the *chanson de geste*, Duggan posits an early period lasting as late as the first half of the thirteenth century, in which poets composed their tales orally and based them on the popular conceptions of historical events. These early poets were more amateurs than jongleurs, 'poets not by profession but by avocation (1989b, 50). As jongleurs assumed the transmission in non-manuscript form of the *chansons de geste*, improvisation continued to play a role, but the practised memories and professionalism of the jongleurs produced a 'drift toward sameness from one performance to the next' (51). Although the technique of composition by theme and formula did allow jongleurs to modify their texts substantially, Duggan envisions them as primarily transmitters of traditional material. All the genres of medieval French literature – the epic, the courtly romance, the saint's life, fabliaux, and the troubadour lyric – constitute a kind of performance axis that ranges from the orally composed (epic) to the entirely memoristic (lyric).

It is difficult to imagine a similarly nuanced understanding of the performance of medieval Spanish literature from the twelfth and thirteenth centuries. There are so few manuscripts from which to draw evidence, minuscule in number compared with the abundance of French vernacular texts. So rich is the French manuscript tradition that the overwhelming evidence for oral composition and vocal performance of this literature is not in the canonical works, but in the many lesser-known texts, mostly unedited since the nineteenth century (Duggan 1989b, 56). In any case, the two phases of oral composition Duggan envisions for the performance of French epic, an initial phase of amateurs improvising their tales, followed by jongleurs whose practised memories led eventually to stable non-manuscript texts, does seem to allow enough divergence to accommodate competing views, as Smith suggested.

Smith's recapitulation virtually closes the door on the argument for the existence of a written Spanish epic created ex nihilo. The extant poems, even if they are thought to be composed in writing, share some degree of the traditional formulaic expression and versification of an autochthonous tradition of narrative poetry, orally composed and performed (Michael 1992, 82). Scholars may ultimately disagree on subsequent points, but there is general consensus regarding the existence of an early stage of the epic, a kind of narrative pre-history similar to that of other epic traditions. This early stage of orally composed narratives shaped the unique artistry of the extant epic poems and continued influencing them even as writing insinuated itself into the process of transmission (Catalán 2001, 372). Scholars do part ways, however, on the question of the precise mode of composition of the extant texts and on the degree to which these texts owe their unique expression to their oral past or their written present.

In general terms, then, the lower percentage of formulas in the Spanish epic as compared to the Yugoslav and the Homeric poems, along with the perception that the *Cid* is an exceptionally sophisticated text, superior to the Yugoslav poems, have led to the conclusion that the extant Spanish epic texts are transitional works, originally elaborated in an oral tradition but at some point appropriated by learned poets who transformed them into works of literature (Montgomery 1977, 92). Fairly early in the process of understanding the implications of Lord's findings for the Spanish epic, Deyermond studied the expressive traits of the *Cid*, including expressions considered formulaic, and concluded that the theme, structure, and style are inextricably linked. Since the Yugoslav epic 'has nothing remotely resembling the wealth of patterns' in the *Cid*, Deyermond finds it 'hard to believe that a poet improvising with the aid of a stock of formulas could have achieved the results I have been describing' (1973, 70–1). His conclusion is later noted and directly challenged in an article included in a collection of essays compiled in Deyermond's honour. John Miletich chose what he considered to be one of the best songs of the South Slavic narrative tradition to determine 'the extent to which the central interest or shaping principle ... informs its structure' (Miletich 1986, 183). Following up on Deyermond's observations of complex aesthetic artistry in the structure and expression of the *Cid*, Miletich found equally compelling patterning in the orally composed *Banović Strahinja*, which he translated from the Serbo-Croatian. Miletich's findings led him to conclude that 'it is not safe to argue for written composition of a particular work on the basis of a highly organized aesthetic structure' (192). Nevertheless, there remains a consensus in the field that the artistry of the *Cid* does not follow from the creative process of oral composition as described by Lord (Montaner 1993, 52–3).

In the case of the *Mocedades* the oral essence of much of its expression (Webber 1980), as well as the prominence of the narrative of Rodrigo's youth in the chronicles and the popular ballad tradition (Armistead 2000, summary 11–12), has convinced scholars that the poem owes much of its essence to an oral narrative tradition (Montgomery 1984b), yet the extant text is thought to have been composed in writing with more or less traditional material as its basis (Funes 2004, lix–lx). In spite of the repeated argument for written composition of the *Cid* based on its artistry, the recognized lack of artistry of the *Mocedades* does not hinder arguments for its written composition (Deyermond 1999, 9). In fact, the poem is a hybrid composition, combining ballad-like passages with others of singular artistry, along with lines of prose and uninspired verse (Montgomery 1984b). Scholars have pointed out for some time that the least poetic passages can be attributed to the disruptive intervention of a learned hand in a pre-existing manuscript (Webber 1980, Montgomery 1984a). Overall, scholars contend that the impoverished expression of the *Mocedades* relative to the artistry of the *Cid* suggests the decline of a robust heroic narrative tradition (Montgomery 1993).

A number of scholars have turned to the inspired work of Paul Zumthor in an attempt to better understand the complex play between writing and orality throughout the Middle Ages. Zumthor describes the medieval world as a time in which an absolute orality existed only among the rural proletariat [*ámbito campesino*], while the art of poetry was practised in more or less proximity to a culture of writing. This situation prevailed between the sixth and sixteenth centuries, engendering two distinct forms of orality: a mixed orality [*oralidad mixta*], where writing exists but is 'externa, parcial y con retraso' [external, partial and lagging behind], and a secondary orality [*oralidad segunda*], where orality 'se constituye a partir de la escritura dentro de un entorno en que ésta tiende a debilitar los valores de la voz en el uso y en lo imaginario' [derives from writing in an environment in which it tends to weaken the value of the voice in practice and in the imaginary] (Zumthor 1989, 20–1).[7] Zumthor allows no strict chronological division between these two types of orality, although he does see as plausible that secondary orality may have become more prominent after the twelfth century. In both forms the voice is the actualizer of the medieval text, a conclusion that leads Zumthor to call for an emphasis on the role of the voice in the interpretation of medieval texts, preferring the term *vocality* to *orality*, whether the text being actualized was composed in writing or orally (21–4).

Following H.R. Jauss, Zumthor proposes an approach to the study of medieval literature that privileges the vocalization of the text, especially in its reception by a listening audience, over its method of production (Zumthor 1989, 26–7). Zumthor does not dismiss the importance of textual production; to the contrary, it continues to be an important consideration: 'Que el texto haya sido o no compuesto por escrito interesa a veces considerablemente a su economía interna y a su gramática' [Whether a text was composed in writing or not may be of considerable interest to its internal economy or its grammar], but

Zumthor is more focused on its mode of reception: 'Pero el hecho de que haya sido recebido a través de la lectura individual directa, o por audición o espectáculo, modifica profundamente su efecto sobre el receptor y consecuentemente su significación' [But the fact that it was received through direct individual reading, or by listening or in performance, modifies profoundly its effect on the recipient and consequently its meaning] (27).

While Zumthor proceeds to explore the implications of the vocalization of medieval texts, Hispano-medievalists reference his call for a new approach, but break no new ground. In what looks like a response to Zumthor's call to emphasize the vocality of medieval texts, Juan Carlos Bayo asks scholars of the Spanish epic to put aside any interest in its mode of composition and focus on its performance as a voiced narrative, to focus on its 'oral condition,' since that is a reality beyond dispute (Bayo 2005, 26). Instead of an enthusiastic call for the exploration of a fresh approach to the epic, Bayo's suggested new focus is actually an expression of his inability to find a way out of the impasse regarding its mode of composition. Alberto Montaner, also echoing Zumthor, cannot seem to find his way out of the impasse either, pointing out that the task of distinguishing between an oral text, especially one composed in memory, as opposed to one composed in performance, and a text written for oral performance, can become a fruitless task, or even 'impertinente' (Montaner 1993, 14; 2007, xciv).

By emphasizing the fruitlessness of distinguishing between texts composed in memory and in writing prior to their oral performance, Montaner stealthily excludes from consideration the role of oral composition. In his view only composition in memory or in writing could explain the expressive, cultural, and literary characteristics of the *Cid*, which he attributes to a highly individualized poet:

> Su formada capacidad poética mueve con fuerza a pensar en un juglar, un profesional de la literatura, si bien uno con cierto nivel de conocimientos jurídicos y un vocabulario con ecos del latín de la iglesia y de los tribunales … En este caso, lo más probable es que, siguiendo las técnicas tradicionales del oficio, hubiese compuesto el texto de memoria, para recitarlo después en voz alta, aunque no pueda rechazarse una composición escrita. Lo que parece totalmente excluido es que estemos ante una improvisación juglaresca copiada al dictado, como – extrapolando el comportamiento de determinados *guslari* serbocroatas modernos – han supuesto algunos oralistas. (Montaner 2007, xciv)

[His learned poetic ability necessarily points to a minstrel, a professional of literature, although one with a certain level of legal knowledge and a vocabulary with echoes of Church Latin and of tribunals … In this case, it is most likely that, following the traditional techniques of the trade, he composed the text in memory, in order to recite it later out loud, although the possibility of a written composition cannot be dismissed. What seems totally excluded is [the possibility] that we are looking at an improvisation by a minstrel copied in dictation, as – extrapolating from the practices of certain modern Serbo Croatian *guslari* – some oralists have supposed.]

This is essentially the same profile and compositional process that Menéndez Pidal imagined for the poet of the *Cid*, which he promoted throughout his extended career and expressed most forcefully in his 1965–6 response to Lord. Like Menéndez Pidal, Montaner rejects the possibility that the *Cid* narrative was in any way improvised (improvisado o repentizado) in the manner of the Serbo Croatian *guslar*. This seems to be a sore point for both scholars, and from my reading of their responses it is the main reason they reject oral composition for the epic in favour of a fixed text, either in memory or in writing. Ironically, Lord emphasizes that improvisation is not an appropriate term for the compositional process employed by the *guslar*: 'If we equate it [oral composition] with improvisation in a broad sense, we are again in error. Improvisation is not a bad term for the process, but it too must be modified by the restrictions of the particular style' (1960, 5).

Lord's study is very clear on the extensive and demanding learning process involved in becoming a singer, and improvisation is not a part of it. A singer 'will say that he was interested in the old songs, had a passion for them, listened to singers, and then, 'work, work, work,' and little by little he learned to sing (24). The learning process comes to an end when the singer has learned enough songs to 'furnish entertainment for several nights' (26). But these songs are not memorized, they are composed in performance using formulaic technique and thematic material, which in the case of the most skilled singer enable him to sing any song he hears and to 'lengthen or shorten a song according to his own desires and to create a new song if he sees fit' (26). Improvisation, if we are to use the term, should be understood as a skill acquired by the best singers through dedication to the learning of traditional poetic expression and themes.

Even though Menéndez Pidal rejects Lord's model of improvisation as a compositional model for the Spanish epic, when he describes what he understands as improvisation, he seems to have something very different in mind:

> Desde este punto de vista, la improvisación tomada como base del poetizar es un jugueteo que sólo prospera en medios de escaso desarrollo intelectual en la técnica artística, sea en grado eminente entre yugoslavos, sea en tono menor entre payadores argentinos, o versadores valecianos o versolaris vascos, capaces de estar horas y horas repentizando en verso sobre cualquier tema. (1965–6, 200)

> [From this point of view, improvisation understood as the basis of composing poetry is an interplay that prospers only in places of scarce intellectual development in artistic technique, whether it is highly considered among Yugoslavs, or of a lesser status among Argentine *payadores* or Valencian *versadores* or Basque *versolaris*, capable of improvising on any subject in verse for hours on end.]

Lord's singers do not improvise on 'any subject'; they are skilled in the formulas and the themes of heroic poetry. Lord's interviews with singers and his recordings of their songs indicate that after hearing a song for the first time they need time to learn it, a day or two, depending on the individual. Although the singers say that they can reproduce a song 'word for word, and line for line' (Lord 1960, 27), Lord's recordings show that the same song sung by two singers is not reproduced word for word, but that they are 'recognizable versions of the same story,' while a song sung by the same singer some seventeen years apart is 'remarkably close to the earlier version' (28), but again, not a verbatim, and therefore memorized, version. Lord also describes literate singers who have composed their songs in writing (129), literate singers who have learned songs by memorizing them from written collections, and illiterate singers who have learned songs read to them from written collections (137). The best singers can learn a song from hearing it read to them, but will make no attempt to memorize it, instead performing it in the traditional way (109). Conversely, the singers who memorize songs are not the true poets; they memorize to compensate for their lack of awareness of the tradition (109). This final point was the most intolerable for Menéndez Pidal, who had spent a lifetime promoting the idea that the Spanish epic poets worked from a fixed text, either in memory or in writing.

From Menéndez Pidal to Montaner, it has become an article of faith among Hispano-medievalists that the Yugoslav model of oral composition is irrelevant to the compositional process of the Spanish epic. The artistry of the Spanish poem is considered superior to the Yugoslav narratives produced through composition by stock formulas and themes (Deyermond 1973, 70–1; Montaner 1993, 13–14), even though Miletich, working with the original-language text, found similarly complex patterning in the orally composed *Boanovic Strahinja*, leading him to conclude that it is not safe to argue for written composition of a particular work on the basis of a highly organized aesthetic structure (Miletich 1986, 192). Miletich's findings reveal a critical flaw in the argument for written composition of the *Cid* based on its artistic superiority over the South Slavic poems recorded by Parry and Lord, made explicit by John Miles Foley in relation to the same critical stance adopted by scholars of the Homeric poems: 'Virtually all scholars who have rendered this vague but summary judgment have consulted the South Slavic works in translation, with little or no experience in the original-language text, never mind of the performances from which those texts derive' (Foley 1999, 41). In Foley's estimation, this 'fundamental shortcoming' disqualifies judgments on the quality of the South Slavic poems, which at best are references to the 'clarity or literary appeal of the English rendering' (41).[8]

The relatively low frequency of formulas in the Spanish epic is another reason used by scholars to reject the oral compositional model for all three extant Spanish epic texts. Yet, the virtual absence of metrical requirements in Spanish epic verse makes the use of formulas less economical than in the Yugoslav and Homeric epics studied by Parry and Lord, in which the strict metrical requirements of the verse necessitated the creation of stock formulas and themes in order to facilitate rapid composition before an expectant audience. From this perspective, the lower frequency of formulas in the Spanish epic does not negate the possibility of its oral composition; it may simply mean that formulas were not as helpful in its oral composition as in the Yugoslav and Homeric epics. We know that not all oral traditions show the universal features of Oral Theory (Foley 1999, 45), the Parry-Lord model of composition in performance utilizing a storehouse of interchangeable fixed expressions, and so we should not discount oral composition as a possibility simply because one or another of the expressive features of the South Slavic poems is not reflected in another poetic tradition. Menéndz Pidal was right on this score – Homer and the *guslari* do represent two starkly distinct worlds, but it does not follow from that fact that their compositions cannot both have been orally composed. As we pursue our inquiry into the compositional process of the Spanish epic, we need to acknowledge that oral traditions are exceedingly heterogeneous, and when we focus on a single tradition, some of its features will be unique to it while others will be shared.

For medieval texts in general, Duggan reinforces our knowledge of the practice among medieval clerics of dictating texts orally to scribes writing on wax tablets for later placement onto parchment (Duggan 2005, 51–7). For the epic, indirect evidence in support of oral composition is found in the examples Duggan cites from the French *chanson de geste* of a kind of improvisation recorded on manuscripts in the course of performance. These examples offer solid evidence that oral performances of romance epics were indeed taken down as dictated texts by scribes, probably first onto wax tablets and later put to parchment (58–61). For the Spanish epic, its most characteristic expressive features have been linked to modern spontaneous speech analysed by the linguist Wallace Chafe (Bailey 2003). In spite of the vast distance between cultures and time, this commonality of expression is readily attributable to the cognitive constraints deployed in narrating events directly to an audience, be they modern researchers or a medieval audience of avid listeners.

Having put to rest in this chapter the major scholarly objections to the possible oral composition of the extant texts of the medieval Spanish epic, the initial results realized through the application of Chafe's findings will serve as a point of departure for a more expansive examination of their expressive characteristics in the chapters that follow. But first, since the placement onto parchment of the extant texts of the Spanish epic is inextricably linked to the learned culture of the time, we shall first explore a variety of learned texts of the period in order to gain a sense of the role of orality in their production.

2 Learned Culture

In medieval Europe *illitteratus* was the term used to denote someone who knew no Latin, while *litteratus* meant that a person knew Latin, or was 'learned.'[1] A parallel antithesis is that of *clericus* and *laicus*, although none of these terms may be used in a strictly modern sense. A monk or cleric might well be *illitteratus* while a knight might in turn be referred to as *clericus*, in the sense of being learned (Clanchy 1979, 177–82). Reading and writing did not go hand in hand as they do today. Literary works were intended for reading aloud, whether in Latin or the vernacular, a practice referred to as *oratio*. Traditional monastic reading, *lectio*, was more a process of savouring the divine wisdom in a book than of finding new ideas or novel information. The ability to put pen to parchment was a specialized skill because it was difficult. This was the practice of scribes, who themselves may not have been *litteratus*. Writing in the modern sense of composition usually was referred to as *dictitare* (literally 'to dictate'). The use of 'writing' (*scriptitare*) is confined to making fair copy on parchment (Clanchy 1979, 216–18).

Thomas Aquinas, one of the most celebrated learned men of the Middle Ages, redacted his texts with varying degrees of oral composition. According to the portrayal offered by Mary Carruthers, Thomas transcribed his early works in a *littera inintelligibilis* [an unintelligible script], writing ostensibly designed not to be read by anyone but the author himself. He would then call his scribes to take down the text in a legible hand while he read his own autograph aloud. When one scribe tired another would take his place. His later works, however, seem to have been dictated completely from memory. This does not mean that Thomas did not consult texts; he did, sometimes asking his scribes to make copies for his use. But the process of composition seems to have occurred once these texts were committed to memory. As one of his scribes attests, his dictation would flow and it 'ran so clearly that it was as if the master were reading aloud from a book under his eyes' (Carruthers 1990, 6).

Other testimonies of medieval composition describe it as an oral process, although revisions followed oral delivery. The twelfth-century preacher Bernard de Clairvaux assumed that his sermons would be easily recalled from one day to the next, but he had them recorded for good measure. His words 'were written down [*scripta*] as they were spoken [*dicta*], that is, recorded by pen [*excepta stylo*].' Bernard's literary production also could occur in 'three phases, composition (*dictare*), transcription (*transcribi*), and publication [*edidi*],' or might include 'oral presentation in small groups [*conferre*], writing out [*scribere*], revisions for correction [*recogitare, corrigere*], and the putting out of an anthology [*legendum praebere*]' (Stock 1983, 409). Eadmer of Canterbury, who wished to conceal from St Anselm the redaction of his biography, was well along in the process of composing on wax tablets and transcribing onto parchment when Anselm asked what it was he ['I'] was composing and copying [*quid dictitarem, quid scriptitarem*] (Clanchy 1979, 218). In the redaction of the miracles of St Foy, Bernard of Angers took accounts from eyewitnesses he interviewed. He hastily scribbled notes that he took with him to Angers 'not to add superfluous information, but to prune repetitions and to rework the whole into a concise, organized literary product' (Stock 1983, 65). As required by canonical procedure there were two texts, the verbal transcript of the testimonies and the later version (*lectio*) composed in Angers.

As these examples demonstrate, in medieval Europe composition of a text involved oral dictation. In the monastic communities where texts were produced, new compositions were based on texts that were familiar to the entire community, and yet their composition did not require the physical presence of a source manuscript. Medievalists have focused a lot of attention on the processes involved in the memorization and subsequent retrieval of texts. Reading a text in order to understand its meaning, the modern-day notion of studying, in the medieval period is known as *lectio*, but to read and assimilate a text, making its meaning one's own, is referred to as *meditatio* (Carruthers 1990, 162). One of the most frequent and longest-lived images for this process is *ruminatio* [chewing the cud], based on the movement of the mouth, *murmur*, that accompanies memorization of a text. Composition is also spoken of as *ruminatio*, in the sense of regurgitation, or in that the readings are collected through *meditatio* and then recollected through *ruminatio* (Carruthers 1990, 165–8). In this imagery there is a dialogue between two minds made possible through the medium of the text. The teachings are read and understood [*lectio*], then assimilated by the reader through *meditatio*; continued rumination later forms the basis for their recollection, and, when deemed fruitful, they later form the basis of a new composition.

The techniques involved in producing a new composition constituted a craft that was learned through the imitation of a master's methods and experience, a process referred to recently as 'monastic rhetoric' (Carruthers 1998, 2–3). It was designed to lead the most adept practitioners to vision, which is understood as 'the activity of composing,' as it 'results in the writing down of an entirely new composition' (183). As Carruthers outlines the practice, it begins with inventive memory work, the reading or recitation of a familiar text. This is followed by fear or dread, a necessary 'compunction' that leads the practitioner into intense meditation or prayer, communion with the divine (a vision or visitation), and finally a return to the everyday world with new knowledge or confidence.

Medieval Spanish literature provides some interesting examples of this rhetorical orthopraxis and its role in the creation of narratives. A marvellous example is the *Poema de Santa Oria*, a vernacular narrative poem on the life of the virgin recluse Oria (Saint Aurea). This work describes the brief life of Oria, especially her visions of heaven. Oria entered the monastery of San Millán de Suso, in the Rioja region of Castile, at age nine and lived there eighteen years as a recluse until her death in the year 1070. The poem also relates how the story of her visions was told by Oria herself to her mother, Amunna (Saint Amunia), also a recluse in the same monastery, who then related it to Munno, a monk who accompanied Oria at the time of her death. Munno later dictated the *Vita beatae Aureae*, a text now lost but identified by Gonzalo de Berceo, the versifier of the *Poema de Santa Oria*, as his source. Berceo put the text to verse in his later years, between 1253 and 1256.

Oria had three visions, but a review of the first one should suffice to illustrate its relevance to the monastic practices described by Carruthers, especially the way in which the vision was inspired by readings, and how these readings in turn formed the basis of a new composition. Oria had her first vision after listening attentively to the reading of the festivity of Saint Eugenia, a virgin martyr from Rome:

25)
Terçera noche era despues de Naujdat
de Sancta Eugenia era festiujdat,
vido de ujsiones vna jnfinidat,
onde pareçe que era plena de sanctidat.[2]
26)
Despues de las matinas, leyda la lection,
escuchola bien Oria con grant deuoçion,
qujso dormir vn poco, tomar consolaçion,
vido en poca hora vna grant vision.
27)
Vido tres sanctas uirgines de grant auctoridad,
todas tres fueron martires en poquiella edat,
Agatha en Catanna, essa rica ciudat,
Olalia en Melerida, njnna de grant beltat.
28)
Cecilia fue terçera, vna martir preçiosa,
que de don Iesu Christo quiso seer esposa,
non quiso otra suegra sy non la Gloriosa,
que fue mas bella que nin lilio nin rosa.

[25) It was the third night after Christmas,
it was the feast of Saint Eugenia,
she saw an infinity of visions,
which means she was full of holiness.
26) After matins, the lesson read,
Oria listened well with great devotion,
she decided to sleep a little, to take consolation,
she soon saw a great vision.
27) She saw three holy virgins of great authority,
all three were martyrs at a young age,
Agatha in Catania, that rich city,
Eulalia in Merida, girl of great beauty.
28) Cecilia was third, a precious martyr,
who decided to be wife to Jesus Christ,
she wanted no other mother-in-law but the Glorious One [Mary],
who was more beautiful than any lily or rose.][3]

As in other visions related in a monastic environment, here the process
starts with a reading, in this case from the life of Saint Eugenia, a

Christian virgin martyred in Rome in the years of Commodus, who reigned from 180 to 192. Like Oria, Eugenia had taken up the monastic life as a young girl. Oria listens to the reading with great devotion and then returns to her cell to sleep and take consolation. The reading must have produced a kind of grief, which explains the desire for consolation. Oria's grief is followed by sleep and her first vision.[4]

In Oria's vision three holy virgin martyrs appear. Like her, all of them are young (27b). The three are alike, dressed of one colour, making it seem that they were all born on the same day. They shone like stars they were so beautiful (29). The three explain that they consider her to be their companion (*compannera*, 32d). The virgins note that Oria delights in reading the stories of their martyrdom; now they want her to understand the heavenly glory and the reward for giving their lives to Christ, as well as show Oria her own golden throne:

33c–d) que subas a los çielos e que ueas que gana,
el seruiçio que fazes e la saya de lana.

34) Tu mucho te deleytas en las nuestras passiones,
de amor e de grado leyes nuestras razones,
queremos que entiendas entre las uisiones,
qual gloria reçibiemos e quales gualardones.

[33c–d) so that you rise to the heavens and see what is earned,
by the service that you do and the wool cloak.
34) You delight greatly in our passions,
with love and pleasure you read our stories,
we want you to understand from the visions,
the glory we received and the rewards.]

The three virgin martyrs who guide Oria relate how she is being led to heaven so that she can understand the rewards of a life of virgin martyrdom, hers as well as theirs. Oria, a devoted reader of their passions, has followed their example on earth and will receive their reward in heaven. The readings have served as a model for Oria's life of virgin sacrifice, and she seems to have turned their lives into hers.

A link between Oria's vision and the texts she loves is made explcit in this passage. This is in line with an essential observation of Carruthers, that the texts familiar to monastic communities are the principal element in the process of inducing communion with the divine. In reference to the *Vision of Wetti*, composed in 894 by the Benedictine abbot Heito of Reichenau, Carruthers states that the visions 'do not come from some unanticipated divine seizure, but are built in a consciously remembered, highly "literary" manner, from the matter he has just been reading' (Carruthers 1998, 182). In the case of Oria, the passions of the three virgin martyrs feed her imagination and desire for martyrdom, and they also link Oria to specific texts. These texts in particular, the narratives of the lives of Saints Eulalia, Cecilia, and Agatha, are initially the source of her vision, which, when narrated by Oria to the monk and confessor Munno, are redeployed in a composition filled with new meaning for both Oria and her monastic community.

A similarly instructive and marvellous example of the role of visions in the process of composition is an episode in the *Historia Silense*. This work has been characterized as a 'deeply problematic text,' due to the uncertainty surounding the origin of the narrative, the principal account of the Leonese monarchy between 1037 and 1072 (Barton and Fletcher 2000, 9). It was once thought to have been composed at the Castilian monastery at Silos, and hence its traditional name, but more recently it has been attributed to a member of the religious community of San Isidro in the city of León, at a date certainly after 1109 and probably before 1118 (13–16). At the centre of the question is precisely the episode that interests us, the translation of the holy relics of Saint Isidore from the Muslim city of Seville to León in the year 1063, during the latter years of the reign of Fernando I. The text, known as the *Translatio Sancti Isidori* and composed 'in or shortly after 1063' (16), was, at some point after its composition, inserted into the *Historia Silense*. For our purposes, it simply offers a shining example of monastic meditational orthopraxis.[5]

Following the English translation of the text, King Fernando I had undertaken a 'campaign against the provinces of Betica and Lusitania ... and laid waste the fields of the barbarians and burned many of their villages.' Benhabet, king of Seville, comes to him offering payment for peace. Part of this payment is a promise to turn over to King Fernando the holy relics of Saint Justa (chap. 95).

An embassy to Seville led by Bishop Alvito meets with Benhabet and is told that the king of Seville does not know the burial site of Justa. This causes Alvito great grief, as he fears that they 'shall return in vain unless divine mercy come to assist the toil of [their] journey.' He asks his company to join him in three days of fasting and prayer, 'so that the divine majesty may deign to reveal the treasure of the holy body which is hidden from us' (chap. 96). On the third day, 'the venerable bishop

Alvito, ever wakeful, was still engaged in prayer. He had sat down briefly to rest his weary limbs as he recited to himself one – I know not which – of the psalms and, on account of the great length of the vigils was overcome by sleep' (chap. 97).

Isidore appears to the bishop in his sleep and explains that God does not wish for the most blessed virgin Justa to be removed, but instead gives his body for translation to León. The bishop wakes and rejoices, 'imploring that if this vision were from God it might be vouchsafed more fully a second and a third time. Praying thus, he fell asleep again' (chap. 98). Isidore appears to the bishop again in a vision, and a third time the bishop wakes, prays, falls asleep, and witnesses a third and final vision. In the third vision Isidore strikes the ground three times with his staff indicating to the bishop the place where the holy treasure lay concealed.

As in the Oria story, there is a concern about authenticity, assuaged in a number of ways. Isidore himself gives bishop Alvito assurances that he is not just an apparition out to trick him. He offers a sign of the truth of his words by promising that soon after his body is brought up to the earth's surface, 'you will be attacked by a grave illness of the body, to which you will succumb; and having shaken off this mortal flesh you will come to us with the crown of righteousness' (chap. 98). The narrator even steps out of the narration to offer an additional detail: 'I speak wondrous things related to me, however, by those who were present. While the search was taking place for the tomb of the blessed body, the tip of the staff with which the holy confessor by his threefold knock had indicated his resting place was found. When it was uncovered [the coffin], so powerful a fragrance was emitted that it drenched the hairs of the head and beard of all who stood by as if with a mist of nectar or the dew of balsam' (chap. 99).

This physical evidence of the presence of Isidore was related to the narrator by those present. It connects the vision of the sleeping bishop to the wakeful world and manifests the divine nature of Isidore by the powerful fragrance his body emits, drenching the hairs of all who stood by, as well as by the discovery of the tip of the staff of the holy confessor. It is also noteworthy that the narrator offers this worldly detail as told by those present, and not by the bishop, who had died in Seville after the recovery of the body of Isidore. In the vision, the bishop's death was foretold as proof that Isidore's words were true. This detail provides an additional parallel to Oria, who, in a subsequent vision, is visited by the Virgin Mary, whom she asks for a sign that she will be saved (strophe 133). The sign Mary promises is a grave illness and death, after which she will ascend into heaven to the seat she had been promised in her first vision (strophes 135–6).

Isidore's body, along with that of the bishop, was taken to León and given honourable sepulchre. Oria's and Amunna's bodies were placed in the same tomb in the monastery of San Millán (strophes 182–3), where the two holy women lived and died, and where the narrative was first spoken by Oria to Munno, written down in a Latin prose text, and put into its final vernacular verse form by Gonzalo de Berceo.[6] These marvellous narrations illustrate the way monastic meditative practice leads to the production of a new composition: a familiar text being read, or recited (a psalm, 'I know not which,' a Saint's life), compunction or dread (the fear of returning to León empty handed, the response to the reading), intense prayer (three days of fasting and prayer, reclusive consolation). In both cases this meditative practice leads to the vision of a venerated saint who reveals God's divine will and provides assurances for the trials ahead, all of which contribute to the formation of a new narrative, the individual components of which were likely familiar from previous readings.[7] In both texts the chain of transmission is explicitly detailed in order to ensure the veracity of the account.

Reading or reciting texts is an important prelude to vision. This literary activity, invariably linked to the absorption of the contents of a book, takes us back to Ezekiel and John, two prophets who were compelled by God to eat a book as a way to internalize the meaning of God's word (Carruthers 1998, 183). A noteworthy later example from Spain is found in the Liber de miraculis Sancti Isidori, attributed to Lucas, before he became bishop of Tuy (d. 1249).[8] Chapters 52–75 of the Liber recount the life and works of Saint Martin of León (Santo Martino in local tradition), a priest and canon regular of the Augustinians. Martin was born in the city of León sometime before 1150 and died there 12 January 1203. He was educated in the monastery of St Marcellus [Sant Marciel] in León and later made pilgrimage to Rome and Constantinople. Returning to Spain he took the religious habit at St Marcellus, but when the monastery was secularized he entered the collegiate church of St Isidore in the same city, where he became brother in habit and community to Lucas.[9] His writings are contained in a two-volume codex labelled Sancti Martini Legionensis opera, first published in four volumes between 1782 and 1786 (cited in Viñayo 1984, 116; Fernández González 1987, 49). It contains a collection of sermons with references to the writings of Saint Isidore, Saint Augustine, the Venerable

Bede, and other medieval thinkers as well as the first written mention in Spain of the writings of the twelfth-century theologian Peter Lombard (Fernández González 1987, 53).

Lucas tells us that although Martin was virtuous in the offices of the church, he was ignorant of the inner meaning of Sacred Scripture and prayed for enlightenment day and night. One night, while in prayer, 'Saint Isidore appeared before him carrying a small book in his hands and said to him: Take this my beloved and eat it, and our Lord God will give you the science of the Sacred Scriptures, for you are known as loyal and just in his house. Likewise I obtained from our Lord Jesus Christ that you be granted anything you ask of God and you will be a partner in the miracles that our Lord God works in this church for me' [apparuit ei b(ea)t(us) doctor Ysidor(us) fere(n)s parvulu(m) libru(m) i(n) manib(u)s and dixit illi: Accipe hunc dilecte mi(hi) and comede and dabit tibi dñs sacram scie(n)ciam scripturar(um), quia fidelis et iustus inve(n)t(us) es in domo eis. Obtinui etiam a dño iesu xpo ut accipias quicq(ui)d a deo petieri et eris co(n)socius miraculor(um) que dñs per me in hac eccl(es)ia op(er)atur] (Viñayo 1984, 12). Isidore then adds that 'the things that the Holy Spirit teaches you, you will be eager to drink for the glory of Christ's name' [et ea que te Sp(irit)us S(an)ct(us) docuerit studebis in gl(or)iam xpi nominis propinare] (13).

Lest we think that Isidore does not mean for Martin to eat the book literally, the narrator goes on to say that because of his simplicity Martin feared that if he did as Isidore commanded, he would break his fast, something strictly prohibited by monastic rule. Isidore, sensing his reluctance to do as commanded, '[t]hen took him by the chin and made him eat the book' [Tunc S(an)ct(us) co(n)fessor accipie(n)s m(en)tu(m) eius libru(m) eu(m) conpulit devorare], after which, Martin 'lit up, looking like a white-hot iron in the fire' [inflamat(us) e(n) totus, ut sibi videretur q(ui) esset quasi ferru(m) candens in igne]. Martin then flourished in his understanding of the Sacred Scriptures, winning debates with teachers of sacred theology, and 'even Jews and heretics could not resist his knowledge and the spirit that was speaking' [Judei q(uo)q(ue) et heretici no(n) poterant resistere sapie(n)tie eius, et spiritui q(ui) loquebant] (Viñayo 1984, 13).

This passage affirms in clear terms the prevailing assumption that texts must be internalized in order to be truly understood and thus useful, as here in debates. The inner knowledge of the Sacred Scriptures is transmitted to Martin through his mouth and stomach, absorbed as it were into his body, a literal depiction of the need to fully absorb the inner meaning of Scripture. Martin's subsequent transformation from a righteous simpleton to a theologian allows him to win debates with teachers of theology and against Jews and heretics, all of which wins him new status. The narrative later describes how Martin's encounter with Isidore and subsequent transformation convinced the abbot of his house to give him licence to hire scribes for writing out his teachings, portraying this too as a consequence of his illumination.[10]

Martin's experience recalls the story of Ezekiel, who was fed the sacred scroll by God and then commanded to go and speak to the House of Israel (3:1–3). It is one of Ezekiel's many visions, and serves to focus Ezekiel on the task Yahweh has reserved for him, which is to deliver God's words to the people of Israel, who had rebelled against God. The prophet John has a similar vision in which God commands him to take the scroll from the hand of the angel of God, and when he asked for it he was told to eat it and 'to prophesy again, this time against many different nations and countries and languages and kings' (Revelation 10:11). These prophetic texts surely form the basis of Martin's vision, yet there is no verbatim correspondence to suggest that Martin was copying either text.[11] Like Ezekiel and John before him, Martin's vision leads to a new composition, the story of his illumination and miraculous transformation preserved in Lucas's text. Martin's story is based on texts he had read and assimilated, as was John's based on his reading of Ezekiel. The assimilation of text is the necessary first step to writing because there can be no composition without a storehouse of texts on which to base it.

Another consideration involved in writing was the expense. Hiring scribes and purchasing the materials for redaction on parchment were expensive propositions. When Martin decided to make his books, his first order of business was to request permission and the necessary resources to carry out his project. For this he addressed himself to his abbot, don Facundo, who after receiving assurances that Martin had the divine knowledge for such an undertaking, [the abbot giving thanks to God, then gave him licence to have the scribes that he wanted for writing his volumes, and to take the offerings of the faithful, from which he could do as he saw fit. Queen Berengaria, when she found out the desire of the saintly man, gave sufficient resources for the holy man to finish his volumes] 'Tunc abbas gr[ati]as age[n]s, dedit ei lice[n]tiam habe[n]di librarios [et] q[ue] uellet uolumina co[n]scribe[n]di, et accipie[n]di hele[m]osinas a fidelib[us], u[n]de posset p[ro]ficere quicq[uo]d sibi meli[us] uideretur. Regina uero bere[n]garia, ut co[m]

perit, desideriu[m] sancti uiri, sufficientes expe[n]sas p[rae]buit ex qui-
bus uir sanctus sua peregit uolu[m]i[n]a' (Viñayo 1984, 32 [ms. chapter
xliiii]). What were these resources? [He had with him daily seven clerics to put together his volumes] 'Habebat igitur secum cl[er]icos septem
cothidie ad sua uolumina co[n]scribenda' (32 [ms. chapter xlv]).

So, the decision to undertake the production of a manuscript text involved considerable expense, and from the narration it is evident that
the decision was not made lightly. The project was so ambitious or unusual that it attracted the attention of Queen Berengalia, daughter of
King Alfonso VIII of Castile, who became queen when she married
King Alfonso IX of Castile and León circa 1198. Part of the reason the
project attracted the patronage of the Queen may have been Martin
himself, especially his miraculous transformation from simpleton to tri-
umphant theologian. Another factor emphasized in the text was the
advanced age at which Martin commenced the writing of his *opera*: [He
could no longer hold up his arms. So he had someone hang ropes to a
beam high up, so that placing them through his shoulders and arms in
such a way that his weak body was suspended, he tolerated its weight
without effort, and in this way writing on wax tablets, he transmitted to
the scribes, who wrote, transferring onto parchment, what by him was
dictated or compiled] 'brachioru[m] suor[um] pondus sustinere no[n]
posset, fecit ad q[ue]ndam trabe[m] in sublimi colligari funes, q[uo]s
p[er] scapullas et brachia ducens quoda[m]modo suspensus inbecillis
corporis pond[us] leuis tollerabat, et sic in tabulis ceratis scribens,
tradebat scriptorib[us], qui ab eo dictata u[e]l copillata scribebant
transfere[n]tes in perg[a]mena' (Viñayo 1984, 29 [ms. chapter lxiii]).[12]

It is not entirely clear from this passage if Martin dictated to himself
as he wrote, compiling passages on wax tablets, or if at times he dictated to the scribes and at other times wrote, compiling passages on
wax tablets (dictata uel co[m]pillata). From the descriptions of the compositional practices of other clerics offered above, we know that both
methods of redacting were common practice, and sometimes used in
combination. In all cases, dictation was a basic component of composition even in such learned environments as the Leonese monastery
where Martin and Lucas de Tuy composed their works. Note how the
word for writing (*scribens, scribebant*) refers solely to the physical act of
inscribing words on a surface, not the same as composing a text, which
here is *dictata* or *co[m]pillata*. For us today, writing involves both organ-
izing our thoughts and putting them on paper, but we conflate the two
in a single word, *writing*.

Of course, texts were also being composed in Spain outside the walls of monasteries, and perhaps the best-known source of manuscript texts was the royal school of translators in Toledo. Here, among the erudite men engaged in the translation of texts from Arabic to Latin, the traditional process of composition was performed orally. Gonzalo Menéndez Pidal offers a detailed description of this process, reconstructed from the prologues, colophons, and the lists of collaborators of the texts themselves. He gives various examples but emphasizes that the process was the same from the time of the founding of the school under Archbishop Raimundus (1126–52). Typically a Jew translated the Arabic text orally into Romance. A second translator, a Christian cleric, hearing the vernacular translation, dictated his Latin translation to a scribe, who wrote it on paper or wax tablets for later preservation on parchment.[13] When Alfonso X began his patronage, he dispensed with the Latin version almost immediately and even experimented with employing a single Jewish translator of the Arabic text into the vernacular Romance. He later returned to the traditional model of two translators, the first a Jew, the second a Christian cleric whose function it was to correct the peculiar expression of the Romance dialect spoken by the Castilian Jews (G. Menéndez Pidal 1951, 367). In all cases, the translations were composed orally and put into writing as dictated oral texts.

Another example of a text being composed in a vernacular language and then translated into Latin is the *Disciplina clericalis* [Instruction for students], the only book of its genre in twelfth-century Latin literature. It contains a series of stories recounted in aphoristic conversations between teachers and students and is designed to impart wisdom (Tolan 1993, 73). What makes the work unique is that its sources are oriental, as the author was born a Jew in Muslim Spain and received en education in Jewish law and Arabic letters. In 1106 as an adult, he converted to Christianity, most likely in an effort to overcome social and professional barriers. For his conversion he changed his name from Moses to Petrus (after the Apostle) Alfonsi (after his godfather, Alfonso I of Aragon). He later migrated north, first to England and then to France, where his learning and writings won him lasting renown. In writing the *Disciplina clericalis*, Petrus tells us that he first composed the text and then translated it into Latin: 'Deus igitur in hoc opusculo michi sit in auxilium qui me librum hunc componere et in latinum transferre compulit' [God then, in this little work of mine be of assistance, who compelled me to compose this book and to translate it into Latin] (Lacarra 1980, 109). It has been assumed that Petrus made his own translation into Latin, composing and translating at the same time (Tolan 1993, 76). Although it is not known in what language Alfonsi originally composed the work, his sources were non-Christian wisdom literature, mostly Arabic, although there appears to be no direct textual link between sources and the *Disciplina* (74–82), suggesting that Petrus composed his work from fables and proverbs he remembered (76). In this case, the process of composition surely involved dictation, if only to himself, because as Petrus composed his text he 'rewrote them in his own words, and forged them into a new and original text' (91).

Oral storytelling continues well into the fourteenth century, as evidenced in the fifty tales that comprise the collection known as *El conde Lucanor*, some of which had appeared previously in the *Disciplina clericalis*. In the closing paragraph of a number of the tales in this collection, the reader is informed that Juan Manuel, nephew of Alfonso X, after hearing that particular story, liked it so well that he 'mandólo escrivir en este libro' [ordered it written down in this book] (cited in Pellen 1998, 190). Juan Manuel surely knew how to write, but was not about to put on the artisan's frock to do so. The *Cid* manuscript is generally viewed as a fourteenth-century copy of a now lost manuscript, including the 1207 date written in the colophon (Montaner 1993, 76–80). It provides the well-known example of Per Abbat, the scribe who 'escrivió este libro' [wrote down this book (manuscript text)].[14]

Of course, the Latin texts of such learned men as Thomas and Martin, or the exempla of Petrus Alfonsi and Juan Manuel, or even the chronicles and prose of the secular elite who took on the task of cultural production in the thirteenth century, bear little resemblance to the expression of the narrative poems of the Spanish epic. Yet they all testify to the fact that producing a text during the medieval period involved speaking, even for the most learned of men. Thomas and Martin were composing texts orally through dictation but based their compositions on written sources they had stored in their memories. In the case of Martin in particular, an entire life lived among books but without writing was transformed by an inspired desire to preserve his sudden and miraculous understanding of sacred texts. Juan Manuel and Petrus Alfonsi seem to have employed exempla from oral and written sources, but their compositions reflect the world of orality in which their stories lived, through dialogues that provide new contexts for these old stories. Juan Manuel, who hoped to instruct the young nobles of the royal court from which he had been excluded, chose to present his exempla through dialogues between a count and his trusted adviser. Petrus, who was conveying oriental wisdom to a Christian audience, did so through dialogues between a teacher and his student. Both formats reflect the oral essence of their sources and their accustomed forms of dissemination, allowing us to understand their use of writing as a response to their personal displacement.

In the case of epic poetry, it seems unlikely that the *juglares* or minstrels of the early thirteenth century, with no known schooling, would be any more inclined than the learned men we have examined to compose their narratives in writing. One way to gauge the degree of orality in the dissemination of a particular narrative is to search out and compare its divergent versions. One of the most compelling examples is found in the narratives related to the battles fought by Charlemagne in northern Spain. Charlemagne was the king who led an army of Franks to an ultimately tragic encounter with the Muslims in the Pyrenean passage known in Spanish as Roncesvalles [Roncevaux], a version of which was immortalized in the *Chanson de Roland*. The existence of this tale is documented in Spain in a brief prose paragraph that summarizes its main events and characters (Alonso 1954, 9). Known as the *Nota Emilianense*, this Latin text was recorded in a codex of the Monastery of San Millán de la Cogolla around 1070, some three decades before the Oxford version of the end of the eleventh century (Duggan 2006, 66). The text dates the battle, 'In era DCCCXVI,' a Spanish dating that corresponds to the year 778 AD and coincides with the date given by the earlier Carolingian annals, such as the *Vita Caroli* (Alonso 1954, 10). The language of the text shows signs of having come from the Romance speakers of Spain (41), and it contains 'essential elements of a literary legend of Roland that probably circulated in oral tradition' (Duggan 2006, 66).[15]

Events similar to those of the *Chanson de Roland* are narrated as historical fact in the two pre-eminent historiographical works written in Latin in thirteenth-century Spain, the *Chronicon mundi* (ca 1236) by Lucas (bishop of Tuy, aka: el Tudense), and the *De rebus Hispanie sive Historia Gothica* (ca 1242) by Rodrigo Jimenez de Rada (bishop of Toledo, aka: el Toledano).[16] For our purposes here, the events of note are the arrival in Spain of Charlemagne and his army, the battle at Roncesvalles, including the death of Roland and the other princes of the Frankish court. In addition to the identification of the vanquished nobles of France, both Spanish histories identify a Spanish Christian warrior responsible for the defeat of the French rearguard, Bernardo del Carpio, nephew of king Alfonso II of Asturias, who fights for independence, for or against his king, depending on the circumstances and, more to the point, on the teller of the tale.

In the narration of Lucas, Charlemagne drives the Muslims out of France, restoring the Christian cult [usque ad montes Pireneos expulsis Sarracenis restituit cultui Christiano]. Charlemagne then traverses the mountains of Roncesvalles [transciectis etiam Roscideuallis montibus] and subjects to his rule the Goths and Spaniards who were in Catalonia and in the mountains of the Basque region [in montibus Vasconie] and in Navarre. Charlemagne writes to Alfonso II of Asturias demanding that he subject himself to the Frankish king, an act that seems to infuriate Bernardo alone. Bernardo rushes with his army to join forces with the Muslims against Charlemagne. Charlemagne lays siege to Tudela, which he later abandons, but conquers Najera and Monte Jardin [monte Iradinum] before initiating his return to France. Marsil, Muslim king of Zaragoza [Saragossa], gathers his army and, together with Bernardo and his Navarrese warriors, attacks the Franks as they are retreating from Spain. As in the *Roland*, Charlemagne had already traversed the pass at Roncesvalles when the Muslims, here led by Bernardo, attacked the rearguard of the French army.

… et cum Francis initio bello Rodlandus, Britannicus prefectus, Anselmus comes, Egiardus, mense Caroli prepositus, cum aliis multis nobilibus Francis exigentibus peccatis nostrorum occisi sunt. Transierat iam quidem Carolus in primo suorum agmine Alpes Rocideuallis dimissa in posterior parte exercitus manu robustorum ob custodiuam, qui Bernaldo, postposito Dei timore, super eos cum Sarracenis accerrime incursante, interfecti sunt. (Falque 2003, 235–6 [Liber IV, cap. 15])

[And having initiated the battle with the French, Roland, prefect of Brittany, count Anselm, Eggihard, overseer of Charlemagne's table, along with many other French nobles were killed paying for our sins. Charlemagne had already traversed with the first of his troops the Roncesvalles Alps, and left the rearguard of his army in the care of the strongest men. Bernardo, having set aside his fear of God and attacking them violently with the Saracens, killed them.]

Charlemagne regroups his army and avenges the massacre of his knights by killing innumerable Muslim nobles 'uiriliter uindicauit ex Sarracenorum nobilibus innumerabilem extinguens multitudinem.' Other events are recounted, but not in anything resembling a coherent narrative. Charlemagne pays homage to Saint James the Apostle by visiting his shrine in Santiago, trekking off the beaten path through Alava 'per deuia Alaue veniens.' Charlemagne returns to Germany taking with him Bernardo, upon whom he bestows great honours ('Carolus autem reuertens in Germaniam secum cum honore magno Bernaldum detulit') (Falque 2003, 236 [Liber IV, cap. XV]). Apart from his narrative of the battle, which is coherent, Lucas seems to be piecing together information from diverse sources.

Bishop Rodrigo narrates the same battle, but with some significant differences. In his version Roland and his fellow nobles, Anselm and Eggihard, are leading the vanguard of Charlemagne's army into Spain: 'In prima acie uenerunt Rollandus prefectus Britannie et Anselmus comes et Egiardus qui erat prepositus mense Caroli' (Fernández Valverde 1987, 127 [Liber IIII, cap. X]) [In the first column came Roland, prefect of Brittany, and count Anselm, and Eggihard, who was overseer of Charlemagne's table]. King Alfonso II and Bernardo attack them straight on and annihilate them. Charlemagne, who was farther back, sensed the destruction ahead of him and sounded the horn he was carrying, calling his men to retreat and regroup. They rushed back to Charlemagne, in part because they were expecting Bernardo and an army of Muslims to attack the rearguard, but Bernardo stayed in the front with Alfonso, destroying the vanguard of the Frankish army:

> Ad eum semianimes audita buccina confugerunt et ad eos qui extrema exercitus obseruabant propter Berinaldum, de quo fama erat quod cum exercitu Arabum per partes Aspe et Seole ueniebat postrema exercitus inuasurus; ipse tamen in strage primorum semper astitit Aldefonso. (Fernández Valverde 1987, 128 [Liber IIII, cap. X])

> [To him they fled half-dead, having heard the horn, and to those who guarded the rearguard of the army from Bernardo, of whom it was rumored that with an Arab army he was coming by way of Aspe and Soule to attack the rearguard, yet he was always with Alfonso slaughtering the vanguard.]

These two versions of an event that is recorded as having taken place nearly five hundred years earlier (778 A.D.), testify to the vigour and credibility of the narrative tradition that kept the story alive. In the early Carolingian annals the attacks came from 'Wascones' or Basques (Alonso 1954, 10 and 32). In the *Nota Emilianense* as well as the *Chanson de Roland* the attackers are the Saracens. In these later versions, the Franks are expelled by Asturians fighting for their independence. In one instance Bernardo and the Muslim king of Zaragoza attack the rearguard of the Franks, in the other Bernardo and his uncle, King Alfonso II of Asturias, do not attack the rearguard, as rumours would have it; instead they strike the vanguard of the Frankish army. Increasingly, the role of the Christian Asturians and their king becomes more heroic. It is not possible to say with certainty if these incremental changes take place in the narrative tradition independently of the chronicler bishop Rodrigo. In the way he tells the story, refuting a popular conception of Bernardo attacking the Frankish rearguard, Rodrigo may in fact be reconstructing history.

Bishop Rodrigo was a contemporary of Lucas and may have been in communication with him as he wrote his *Chronicon mundi* (Linehan 2002, 33–8). Because of the compelling nature of the story of the Franks' invasion of Spain, we can say with a fair amount of certainty that the story Rodrigo refutes is the one told by jongleurs, and also reported by Lucas. In fact, Rodrigo says as much when he addresses the reports of other feats attributed to Charlemagne:

> Non nulli histrionum fabulis inherentes ferunt Carolum ciuitates plurimas, castra et oppida in Hispaniis acquisisse multaque prelia cum Arabibus strenue perpetrasse et stratam publicam a Gallis et Germania ad Sanctum Iacobum recto itinere direxisse. (Fernández Valverde, 1987, 128 [Liber IIII, cap. X])

> [Some, adhering to the stories of the jongleurs, affirm that Charlemagne had won many cities, castles, and towns in Spain and he had vigorously perpetrated many battles against Arabs, and he set the public road in a straight line from Gaul and Germany to Santiago.][17]

In this instance, as in the case of the attack by Bernardo directly into the vanguard of the Franks, Rodrigo mentions his legendary sources only to refute them. He then enumerates all the conquests of cities by Spanish kings in the last two hundred years and affirms that he cannot see how Carlos could have conquered any of these cities since some four hundred years had passed since his death. This leads him to conclude:

> Facti igitur euidencie est pocius annuendum quam fabulosis narrationibus atendendum. Siue enim a Christianis, siue a Sarracenis ipse uel eius

exercitus fuit uictus, itinere retrogrado comitatus dampnis et periculis retrocessit, nec stratum Sancti Iacbi suo itinere potuit publicare, cui non obuenit transitum Vallis Rocide penetrare. (Fernández Valverde 1987, 130 [Liber iiii, cap. XI])

[It is better to accept the evidence of the facts than to pay heed to the legendary stories. Whether by Christians or by Saracens [Muslims], he or his army was vanquished, he returned from whence he came with ruin and suffering for company, nor could he open the route of Saint James [Santiago] on his march he who did not manage to get through Roncesvalles.]

The Alfonsine chroniclers struggle to blend the two earlier Latin versions, but their best effort in managing the variant narrations is to intersperse them as the narrative progresses from one episode to another.[18] The frustration is palpable, and when the translators come across references to unreliable tales, they add their own perspective on oral narratives to the mix:

Et algunos dizen en sus cantares et en sus fablas de gesta que conquirio Carlos en Espanna muchas çipdades et muchos castiellos, et que ouo y muchas lides con moros, et que desenbargo et abrio el camino desde Alemannia fasta Sanctiago. Mas en verdat esto non podria ser, fueras tanto en Catalonna conquirio Barçilona, Gironda, Ausona et Urgel con sus terminos; et lo al que chufan ende non es de creer. (Here follows a long list of documented conquests by Christian kings of Spanish cities from the Muslims.) Todas estas conquistas fueron fechas de dozientos annos aca. Pues non veemos nin fallamos que Carlos ganase ninguna cosa en Espanna, ca bien a quatroçientos annos que el murio, onde mas deue omne creer a lo que semeja con guisa et con razon de que falla escritos y recabdos, que non a las fablas de los que cuentan lo que non saben. (Menéndez Pidal 1906, 355–6)

[And some say in their songs and in their (spoken) tales of deeds that Carlos conquered in Spain many cities and many castles, and that he had there many battles with Moors, and that he cleared and opened up the (pilgrimage) route from Germany to Santiago. But truthfully this could not be, except for in Catalonia he conquered Barcelona, Gerona, Osona and Urgel and their surroundings; and the other ones they make up are not to be believed. (Here follows a long list of conquests by Christian kings of Spanish cities from the Muslims.) All these conquests were made within the last two hundred years. We do not see or find that Carlos took anything in Spain, for it has been a good four hundred years since he died, thus man should more believe what seems to be right and well reasoned, which he finds written and explained, than the spoken tales of those who say what they do not know.]

The vernacular text is essentially a translation of bishop Rodrigo's text, although the distrust of the oral tales is livelier and more palpable. In later chapters the Alfonsine chroniclers take note of other epic narratives directly from the *juglares* and continue to express ambivalence about their oral sources, especially when these contradict written accounts of the same events (Menéndez Pidal 1924, 368–70). In retrospect, it should be noted that the written versions of the heroic tales so admired by the Alfonsine chroniclers, such as those of the *Chronicon mundi* and the *De rebus Hispanie* noted above, also employed the narratives of *juglares* as their principal source.

Regarding the Cid, there are two notable Latin texts that celebrate his deeds and fame prior to the extant epic poem, and another in which the legend of the Cid is mentioned in passing. In part because the texts are unattributed, the dates and therefore their sequence are open to question. Alberto Montaner has argued for seeing them collectively as representative of a '*boom* literario sobre el héroe burgalés' [literary boom on the hero from Burgos] in the final quarter of the twelfth century, beginning with the composition of the *Historia Roderici* (Montaner and Escobar 2001, 119). Montaner's linking of these texts in a literary movement represents a break from previous scholarship, which saw each text as a unique phenomenon, determined by unique historical and personal circumstances. It is a bold concept, but here we are going to follow a different chronology, one which assumes that the enthusiasm for the deeds of Rodrigo Díaz began in his own lifetime, and not as part of a literary boom occurring spontaneously some seventy-five years after his death.

The first of the Latin works on the Cid is a brief and incomplete poem known as the *Carmen Campidoctoris*, or Poem of the Campeador (another name for the Cid, meaning Victor or Battler). It is preserved in a unique manuscript from the thirteenth century (Paris, Bibliothèque Nationale, lat. 5132), probably composed by a monk of the Catalonian monastery of Ripoll (Gil 1990, 102). There are varied opinions regarding its date of composition, but the editor of the Latin edition supports the arguments for an early date (ca 1083) and its composition by a cleric well versed in rhetorical topics (101). This dating situates the composition of the poem during the lifetime of Rodrigo Díaz, and even before his conquest of the Moorish kingdom of Valencia, his most famous feat.

The poem is narrowly focused on recollecting a series of confrontations between the Cid and his individual adversaries. It consists of thirty-two strophes of four verses each, composed in what have been termed Sapphic verse, although the poet is counting syllables and not feet (eleven syllables in the three Sapphic lines and five in the Adonic), with a regular caesura after the fifth syllable. Pitch is ignored in place of accentual stress, which falls on the fourth and tenth syllables, and most times also on the first, in the Sapphic lines, and on the first and fourth syllables in the Adonic (Montaner and Escobar 2001, 148–9). Also noteworthy for our present purposes, the four lines of each strophe bear assonance on the unstressed final syllable, as exemplified here in the opening strophe, 'Gesta bellorum possumus referre Paris et Pyrri necnon et Eneae, / Multi poetae plurima cum laude / Que conscripsere' [We may speak of warrior deeds / of Paris and Pyrrhus and even Eneas / that many poets in highest praise / composed] (Gil 1990, 105).[19] The poem has a learned flavour, exemplified here in its reference to classical literature, but its subject ('Roderici principis bella,' from lines 7–8) and its prosody reflect an affinity with an as-yet undocumented vernacular epic on the Cid, especially in its use of caesura, end-line assonance, and syllabic as opposed to quantitative versification.

Another indicator of the presence of a vernacular narrative as an inspiration for the Latin poem can be found in its title. In the fifth strophe the poet calls out to the people to come hear the poem of the *Campeador*, 'Eia, letando, populi caterue, / Campidoctoris hoc carmen audite' [Gather round, you throngs of people, in celebration, / to hear this poem of the Campeador] (lines 17–18). *Campidoctor* [*Campeador*] is a reference to Rodrigo Díaz, as the poem soon explains. When young Rodrigo defeated a Navarrese warrior in single combat, his superiors started calling him *Campidoctor*, 'Cum adolescens deuicit Nauarrum, / Hinc Campidoctor dictus est maiorum / ore uirorum' [as an adolescent he defeated the Navarrese, henceforth he was called Campidoctor from the mouths of the high-ranking men] (lines 26–8).[20] This use of *campidoctor* does not seem to correspond to its classical meaning of 'drill master'; instead it is more akin to the vernacular epithet *Campeador*, meaning 'victor' or 'battler,' and employed regularly in the *Cid* (Montaner and Escobar 2001, 26–34, 137–43). Given that *Campidoctor* is used to call the people's attention to the poem, albeit rhetorically, the poet must have expected that his audience would know the subject, as he makes clear in an earlier verse, 'Magis qui eius freti estis ope, / cuncti uenite' [Especially those of you confident in his (the Campeador's) strength, / come all] (lines 19–20). From these passages it seems reasonable to conclude that a vernacular narrative on the Cid, employing the same epithet as the extant poem, was circulating at the time and that the author of the Latin poem was inspired by its popularity to write his learned version of Rodrigo's principal combats.

Soon after the death of the Cid, a Latin biography known as the *Historia Roderici* emerged.[21] It is currently extant in three manuscripts, all housed in the Biblioteca de la Real Academia de la Historia in Madrid, Spain (Falque 1990, 25–8). The prose text narrates in detail the trials and triumphs of the later life of Rodrigo Díaz, including a fairly obsessive focus on his attempts to resolve differences with king Alfonso VI, and his triumphal conquest and subsequent rule of the Moorish kingdom of Valencia in 1094. It has long been considered the principal source for the historical, as opposed to the legendary, life of the Cid (Barton and Fletcher 2000, 91).

In the determination of a possible author and sources, Menéndez Pidal and subsequent scholars have imagined a possible Cidian archive preserving documents related to the Cid's exploits, mostly as a way to explain the historical accuracy of the events narrated and what seems to be the inclusion of documents verbatim in the narrative (Barton and Fletcher 2000, 92 and 97). Montaner rejects as anachronistic for the eleventh and twelfth centuries the possibility that the *Historia* could have as its source written documents stored in a putative Cidian archive, and instead stresses oral sources: 'se ha de suponer que [el autor] se basó, siquiera fuese parcialmente, en relaciones de terceros, orales o menos probablemente escritas. Y si fue así en parte, nada impide que lo haya sido en todo' [one must assume that the author based his work, even if it was partially, on second-hand stories, oral or less probably written. And if it was that way in part, nothing impedes it from being entirely so] (Montaner and Escobar 2001, 83).

As support for this understanding of the genesis of the written text, there is no higher authority than the opening paragraph of the *Historia* itself. In it the author first states that [because the actions of this world, in the immense and ceaseless passing of years, if they are not fixed in writing, are doubtless consigned to oblivion] 'Quoniam rerum temporalium gesta, inmensa annorum uolubilitate pretereuntia, nisi sub

notificationis speculo denotentur, obliuioni proculdubio traduntur,'
and then explains that [for that reason, we resolved to have and to preserve under the light of the written word the family of that most noble
and warlike man, Rodrigo Díaz, and the battles heroically fought by
him] 'idcirco Roderici Didaci, nobilissimi ac bellatoris uiri prosapiam,
et bella ab eodem uiriliter peracta, sub scripti luce contineri atque ha-
beri decreuimos' (Falque 1990, 47). It seems quite clear from this statement that the author of the *Historia* was not working from written
sources, and that he was unaware of their existence. Consequently, and
in accordance with Montaner, his sources must have been oral.[22] These
oral sources may well have included early versions of a vernacular epic
poem circulating orally at the time, especially since some episodes in
the *Historia* are later narrated in the *Cid*.[23]

A final reference to an emerging vernacular epic on the Cid is a mention of the Cid in the Latin *Poema de Almería*, a lengthy narrative poem
that comes at the end of the second book of the *Cronica Adefonsi
Imperatori* [Chronicle of the Emperor Alfonso] VII of León-Castile
(1126–57). The poem consists of 385 and a half lines of rhythmic hexam-
eters on the conquest of Almeria in 1147 by Alfonso VII and his allies (ca
1148).[24] The poem is incomplete, but of interest to us is the following
mention of Rodrigo, the Cid: 'Ipse Rodericus, Meo Cidi saepe vocatus,
/ de quo cantatur quod ab hostibus haud superatur, / qui domuit
Mauros, comites domuit quoque nostros' [Rodrigo himself, often called
Mio Cid, / of whom it is sung that he was not defeated by enemies, /
who dominated Moors, also dominated our counts] (Salvador Martínez
1975, 38 [lines 220–2]).[25] Mio Cid is of course the most common epithet
for Rodrigo Díaz in the extant vernacular poem, although it was probably also a name he used in real life. But these lines do affirm that his
deeds were sung, and it seems clear that the poet and the audience of
this poem, composed some fifty years after the death of Rodrigo in
1099, knew of the Cid's life from song.

Interestingly, then, these learned texts help confirm the existence of
an oral narrative tradition of epic deeds. Yet the fact that only two vernacular epic poems were ever preserved in writing may be seen as a
clear indication that writing was not the most common form of convey-
ance for narrative poetry. Writing was the manner in which religious
texts were conveyed, and yet even these involved some degree of oral
composition, although subsequent editing was surely employed as a
means to render the original dictation into a prose form that was familiar to its learned audience. Epic narratives would also have been

dictated orally as part of the process of placing them onto parchment, yet there was probably little concern on the part of the scribes to alter the expression of the poets, since they would have had no training to help them with that task. Nevertheless, these poems do reveal varying degrees of learned influence, and in the next three chapters this study will examine the manner in which the expression of the *Cid*, the *Fernán González*, and the *Mocedades* reflects the oral world of their origin, and the extent to which their transfer to parchment imbued them with learned tendencies.

3 The *Cantar de Mio Cid*

In the previous chapter we saw that in the Middle Ages in general, and in the thirteenth century in particular, oral composition was an integral part of the process of writing texts in Latin. In some cases, the texts were first composed in the vernacular and then translated into Latin.[1] Texts composed in the vernacular required no translation, of course, since the same language is used for composing and for recording the text. The first of the extant vernacular epic texts preserved in Christian Spain is the *Cantar de Mio Cid*, put to parchment in 1207 in a process that must have included at least the same degree of oral composition as employed in the production of Latin texts. It follows, then, that seeing the act of preserving the *Cid* on parchment as anything but a continuum involving speech and writing is inappropriate for the period.[2] The question then becomes, how much of the *Cid* is composed orally, and how much of it is the result of writing? What I propose in this chapter is to situate the poem in its proper context, and then to employ findings from a variety of scholars, but most especially from the field of discourse analysis, in order to pinpoint the oral expression in some of the best-known passages in the poem.

It is clear enough from a reading of the *Cid* that knights were the power brokers of society. They lived in a predominantly oral world; even those among them who were considered experts on legal matters, *los sabidores* or *coñoscedores* (vv. 3070, 3137), are depicted practising their craft orally. They had to be adept at expressing themselves in speech in order to rule over their fellow men, and there can be no doubt that status is reflected in speech and that good speech coupled with high status sustain power and authority. There are specific indicators of the importance given to good speech in the poem, such as when the Cid congratulates Minaya on speaking well in counsel over the next course of action to take in the defence of Alcocer: 'A mi guisa fablastes, / ondrásteisvos, Minaya, ca avérvoslo iedes de far' (vv. 677b–678) [You spoke to my liking, / you honoured yourself, Minaya, just as you were bound to do]. The first time the Cid speaks in the poem he does so 'bien e tan mesurado' (v. 7) [well and so measured]. Likewise, when Asur González, the older brother of the malicious Infantes de Carrión, enters the king's court in Toledo, it is not only his drunken appearance that exemplifies the decadence of his family, but his speech as well: 'Asur Gonçález entrava por el palaçio, / manto armiño e un brial rastrando, / vermejo viene, ca era almorçado, / en lo que fabló avié poco recabdo' (vv. 3373–6) [Asur González entered the palace, / dragging his ermine fur and his tunic, / he's all red, for he had just eaten, / in what he said there is little prudence]. Additional and more nuanced indicators of the esteem attached to good speaking in the *Cid* are the subtle hierarchies of speech employed in the hortatory modes (Montgomery 1998, 97–112).

We know that in the monasteries and in the royal courts writing was taking place. The poem is available to us today because it was put into writing, probably at the Castilian monastery of San Pedro de Cardeña (Bailey 2003, 266). There are two references to writing in the poem – 'Antes de la noche, en Burgos d'él entró su carta' (v. 23) [Before nightfall, his letter entered Burgos]; 'Meterlos he en escripto e todos sean contados' (v. 1259) [I will put them in writing and let them all be counted] – although overall the poem is clearly attuned to a speech-centred world. In order to better understand the oral basis of the expression in the poem, we will turn our attention to a field of linguistics that has made good use of the findings of cognitive psychology and discourse analysis to distinguish between written and oral expression. The work of Wallace Chafe, in particular, has proven to be especially pertinent in this regard and has shed light on the cognitive basis for the highly stylized expression of Homeric discourse (Bakker 1997, 35–53), as well as providing insights into the oral foundation of Spanish epic discourse (Bailey 2003).

Chafe and his collaborators are best known for a study they conducted that was designed to probe the way people talk about things they have experienced and later recall. They first produced a short film, which they later showed to different groups of people. They then conducted individual interviews in which the subjects were asked to narrate through recall the action in the film. The recording and transcription of those interviews, in which everyone produced a 'spontaneous and reasonable description of what the film contained' (Chafe, ed. 1980, xv), constitute the data on which their subsequent studies are based. Chafe used the data to probe the link between consciousness and the expressive characteristics of the spontaneous speech of his subjects as they narrated the action of the film. Chafe found that among the most salient characteristics of this spontaneous speech is its production in relatively brief spurts. He initially refers to these spurts of speech as 'idea units,' a term already in use which highlights their resemblance to single clauses (Chafe 1980, 13). In his subsequent work Chafe prefers to call them 'intonation units,' a reflection of the importance he attributes to their single intonation contour (Chafe and Danielwicz 1987, 10).

In cognitive terms, these units 'express what is in the speaker's short-term memory or "focus of consciousness," at the time [they are] produced' (Chafe and Danielwicz 1987, 10). The prototypical intonation unit has the following properties: 1) it is spoken with a single, coherent intonation contour; 2) it is followed by a pause; and 3) it is likely to be a single clause. Chafe studies some properties of intonation units and finds that 'a speaker does not, or cannot, focus on more information than can be expressed in about six words,' while their syntax 'must be kept simple' (10). He concludes that intonation units are the natural unit of speech, while sentences have become the major unit of writing. This distinction comes about 'presumably because writers have the leisure to perfect complex and coherent sentence structures which speakers are moving too fast to produce' (18).

Egbert Bakker has associated the cognitive concept of the intonation unit with the highly stylized and rhythmically sophisticated Homeric verse. He finds that, just as in ordinary speech, the basic metrical unit of Homeric verse is not the sentence but the intonation unit. The intonational and prosodic properties of this unit of speech are stylized into metrical properties, their cognitively determined length making them the ideal basis for formulas as the basic ingredients of epic discourse. The metrical requirements of Homeric verse would not exclude it from being considered a form of speech. In Bakker's terminology it is 'special speech' (Bakker 1999, 37–9). In the Spanish epic, where there are essentially no metrical properties, the cognitive relation between narrative discourse and Chafe's concept of the intonation unit should be even more evident than in Homeric poetry.

Initially, the similarities between Chafe's intonation units and epic verse may not be immediately apparent to readers of modern editions of the *Cid*. Following the lead of the manuscript text, modern editors represent the poem as a series of verses whose length is determined by their end-line assonance. This rhyme pattern is based on the repetition of the same stressed or tonic vowel in the final word of each verse, as in lines 1077–81, cited below (and<u>a</u>r, atr<u>á</u>s, repintr<u>á</u>, h<u>a</u>, algu<u>a</u>ndre). When the stress falls on the penultimate vowel, as in the first five lines of the poem (llor<u>a</u>ndo, cat<u>a</u>ndo, cañ<u>a</u>dos, m<u>a</u>ntos, mud<u>a</u>dos), the final unstressed vowels of the series (in this case <u>o</u>) almost always match as well (Montaner 2005, 165–7). Editors also divide each verse into two half-lines or hemistichs, by inserting a space between what they judge to be two clauses. This action is based on the assumption that the narrator would pause after each clause, although in the manuscript there is no indication of any pause. The number of syllables in Spanish epic verse is not regular, as in alexandrine verse, nor are the verses measured in feet, as in Homeric verse. There is essentially no uniform length to these verses, although it has been observed that no hemistich can contain more than eleven syllables because this would require an additional caesura, the term used to designate the pause between half-lines or hemistichs (Montaner 2005, 257). Modern editors also take the liberty of identifying sequences of verses with the same assonance, referred to as a *laisse* (Fr.) or *tirada* (Sp.), and assigning them a number. In the Spanish epic these *tiradas* vary greatly in length, from a minimum of two verses to over two hundred. Changes in assonance are attributed to transitions in the narration, with a sub-category of non-starters (*versos sueltos*) brought about by something called 'deictic dissonance' (Bayo 2001, 86–7).

Even though the lines of the poem are counted in verses, the hemistich is considered the basic component of epic verse (Montaner 1993, 37). It corresponds closely to Chafe's intonation unit, which he considers the basic unit of speech, normally consisting of four to six words each, followed by a pause, and likely to be a single clause (Chafe and Danielwicz 1987, 10). Let us look at a specific passage from the *Cid* for confirmation of this similarity, presented here as in the manuscript text:

Aguijava el conde e pensava de andar,
tornando va la cabeça e catándos' atrás,
miedo iva aviendo que Mio Çid se repintrá,
lo que non ferié el caboso por cuanto en el mundo ha,
una deslealtança ca non la fizo alguandre. (vv. 1077–81)[3]

[The Count set spur and he began to ride,
he keeps turning his head and [he keeps] looking back,

he is feeling afraid that Mio Cid will take it back,
which the worthy one would not do for anything in the world,
a disloyal act, for he never did it.]

As noted above, modern editors separate what they assume are two
clauses in each line with a space that is meant to represent a natural, as
opposed to a metrical, pause, or caesura, as follows:

Aguijava el conde   e pensava de andar,
tornando va la cabeça   e catándos' atrás,
miedo iva aviendo   que Mio Çid se repintrá,
lo que non ferié el caboso   por cuanto en el mundo ha,
una deslealtança,   ca non la fizo alguandre. (Montaner 1993, 165 [lines
    1077–81])

In cognitive terms, these hemistichs 'express what is in the speaker's
short-term memory or "focus of consciousness," at the time [they are]
produced' (Chafe and Danielwicz 1987, 10). The poem progresses
through the use of what has come to be known as the string-along or
additive style, also known grammatically as parataxis, which typically
produces repetitions as the narrator expands on statements he has just
made. This is common in speech because in speaking there is little possibility of synthesis, just the continuous production of brief spurts of
speech focused on conveying single acts and thoughts that in time add
up to a scene, an episode, and eventually a story. In this process, when
a clarification needs to be made, the speaker must return to his original
thought by repeating it, and then offer his clarification or expansion.

Following Chafe's transcriptions of spontaneous speech (Chafe 1996,
40–1), we can also represent these hemistichs (intonation units) in the
following way:

1 Aguijava el conde
2 e pensava de andar,
3 tornando va la cabeça
4 e catándos' atrás,
5 miedo iva aviendo
6 que Mio Çid se repintrá,
7 lo que non ferié el caboso
8 por cuanto en el mundo ha,
9 una deslealtança,
10 ca non la fizo alguandre.

In this representation of the lines we can better appreciate the relationship between Chafe's concept of 'brief spurts of speech' and the clausal structure, seeing them both as formed by the cognitive limitations of the oral narrative process. Unable to focus on more than one thought or image at a time, the narrator must first describe the count's physical actions (lines 1–4), then proceed to inform us of what the count was thinking while he was acting in that fashion (lines 5–6). The narrator then changes his plane of thought from what the count is thinking to his own response to it. In doing so he offers a characterization of the Cid, and of the count, by telling us that the Cid (unlike the count) would never do such a thing (line 7), and qualifies that affirmation (line 8). The narrator then must restate what he is talking about (una deslealtança, line 9), presumably because the third-person neuter pronoun (lo que non farié el caboso, line 7) is not especially clear, but also as an aid to shifting his thoughts from the hypothetical realm (non farié) to the real (que non la fizo alguandre), and to finally affirm the Cid's moral character through his actions (line 10). Modern readers of the poem know that this final progression is needed because deeds must confirm words, and in this particular instance, the Cid cannot perform a disloyal act; he can only not have done it, ever.

If this passage were written and then memorized for oral performance, as most scholars of the Spanish epic believe, there would be a synthesis of expression equivalent to written discourse. This is not the case, and instead of synthesis, the poet first tells us of the count's actions and then narrates separately the thinking behind those actions. The poet first states that the Cid would never do that ('lo que' is the equivalent of a relative pronoun), referring back to the count's fear that the Cid might change his mind (que Mio Çid se repintrá), before specifying what he meant (una deslealtança), and then in a separate statement affirming that he never did it, maybe as a kind of concrete proof of his previous assertion that he would never do it. As we listen to the poem, and generally as we read it as well, there is the sense that the language flows smoothly. But when we examine it closely we see that the language comes in short spurts, giving it an intermittent quality, and that the poet is simultaneously narrating and clarifying, moving back and forth from thought to action as the narrative progresses.

This expressive feature might be attributed to the binary structure of two hemistichs per verse, with assonance lending a finality to each verse, especially the closely related reiterations of actions that at first blush seem to serve more to complete the verse than to add anything new (Aguijava el conde e pensava de andar, / tornando va la cabeça e catándos' atrás). But actions and thoughts are intimately related in the poem, and the actions and thoughts of the count reflect on the Cid, whose actions (and the thoughts of the poet about the Cid's actions) also reflect on the count. The progression is slow but deliberate; the narrative must move forward for the audience, but at the same time the narrator is limited in what he can say in each one of his brief spurts of speech. Chafe found something similar in his data: 'very few if any cases in which there are two or more separately activated new ideas within the same intonation unit,' which to him suggests the hypothesis that 'an intonation unit can express no more than one new idea,' and that thought 'proceeds in terms of one such activation at a time, and each activation applies to a single referent, event, or state, but not to more than one' (Chafe 1994, 109). Equally meaningful for our understanding of oral poetry is Chafe's sense that this limitation on what the speaker can say may also be assumed for the listener, that neither one can 'handle more than one idea at a time' (109).

The similarities between Chafe's intonation unit and the hemistichs of the *Cid* suggest that both may be understood as cognitively based units of speech. Chafe found in spontaneous speech a clause-final intonation contour, a slight rise in pitch, which he indicates with a comma, and a slight fall in pitch, which he indicates with a period. These units are also separated by brief pauses, and their syntax is simple, often beginning with the word 'and,' or another simple conjunction, such as 'but' or 'so' (Chafe 1980, 14). The scribes of the manuscript text of the *Cid* wrote down the poem in verses, which is assumed to be in recognition of its end-line assonance. Modern editors separate each verse into two half-lines in recognition of an assumption that after each hemistich the poet pauses. The intonation contour of epic verse is not available to us for analysis, but we may speculate that after every half-line a change in pitch occurred; perhaps the first would be a rise and the second a fall as with the spontaneous speech recorded by Chafe. In any case, the scribe who put the poem to parchment does not separate the hemistichs, nor does he group verses by their common assonance, suggesting that any changes in pitch were considered part of natural speech, and not something to be identified in the manuscript text. Clearly, end-line assonance marked the end of one verse and the beginning of another, but not a metrical principle.

Another unique feature of epic verse is its string-along style, or parataxis. This has long been considered a marker of orally composed poetry (Duggan 2005, 62), and linguists have affirmed that paratactic syntax is indeed characteristic of spoken discourse, and that spontaneous or novel speech is typically delivered 'one clause at a time' (Chafe 1980, 30). Furthermore, the one-clause-at-a-time processing of spontaneous or novel discourse is not a style at all, but a constraint on speakers in which 'the largest unit of novel discourse that can be fully encoded in one encoding operation is a single clause of eight to ten words' (Pawley and Syder 1983, 202). When a speaker begins to narrate a stretch of novel discourse over several clauses, only the first few words are known. By generating one clause at a time, as opposed to integrating or subordinating clauses, a speaker 'can maintain grammaticality and semantic continuity because his clauses can be planned more or less independently, and each major semantic unit, being only a single clause, can be encoded and uttered without internal breaks' (203).

Deyermond, without recourse to these linguistic findings, suggested that parataxis is not proof of oral composition, but of oral diffusion only (1987, 42n3).[4] Because he gives nothing in the way of proof or explanation, it is difficult to address his assertion. He seems to be suggesting that the paratactic syntax of the epic is a style chosen by a writer who has in mind the need of the minstrel to memorize the poem. The writer then would choose to employ a paratactic style, refraining from enjambment, in order to facilitate the memorization of the poem. If so, then the fourteenth-century *Proverbios morales* would serve as a compelling counterpoint to his assertion. This is a poem that we know was written by a learned author, that employs enjambment as well as integrated or subordinate clauses, and yet it circulated widely in oral form (Díaz-Mas and Mota 1998, 20–6).

The minimal metrical requirements of Spanish epic verse should help to make the cognitive relationship between epic narrative discourse and Chafe's concept of the intonation unit even more evident than in the highly metrical Homeric poetry studied by Bakker. The clause-like hemistichs and paratactic verse of the epic can be readily understood in terms of Chafe's intonation unit, a single focus of consciousness, adjoined to subsequent, cognitively based spurts of speech. Another passage from the *Cid* can help to reinforce the similarity, as well as introduce an additional aspect of narrative formation brought to light by Chafe. The passage is from the well-known 'niña de nuef años' [nine-year-old girl] episode.

15   Mio Çid Ruy Díaz por   Burgos entrava,
     en su conpaña   sessaenta pendones,

16*b*   exiénlo ver   mugieres e varones,
       burgeses e burgesas   por las finiestras son,
       plorando de los ojos,   tanto avién el dolor,
       de las sus bocas   todos dizían una razón,
20   –¡Dios, qué buen vassallo,   si oviesse buen señor!–
       Conbidarle ien de grado,   mas ninguno non osava,
       el rey don Alfonso   tanto avié la grand saña,
       antes de la noche,   en Burgos d'él entró su carta,
       con grand recabdo   e fuertemientre sellada,
25   que a Mio Çid Ruy Díaz   que nadi nol' diessen posada,
       e aquel que ge la diesse   sopiesse vera palabra,
       que perderié los averes   e más los ojos de la cara,
       e aun demás   los cuerpos e las almas.
       Grande duelo avién   las yentes cristianas,
30   ascóndense de Mio Çid,   ca no l'osan dezir nada.
       El Campeador   adeliñó a su posada,
       assí commo llegó a la puerta,   fallóla bien çerrada,
       por miedo del rey Alfonso,   que assí lo avién parado,
34   que si non la quebrantás por fuerça,   que non ge la abriesse nadi.
          (*Cid*, vv. 15–34)

[15   Mio Cid Ruy Díaz entered Burgos,
       in his company sixty pennons,
16*b*   women and men came out to see him,
       burghers, men and women, are at their windows,
       weeping from their eyes, they had such sorrow,
       from their mouths all said one thing,
20   'God, what a good vassal, if he had a good lord!'
       They would welcome him gladly, but none dared,
       King don Alfonso had such terrible anger,
       before nightfall, his letter reached Burgos,
       with much precaution and heavily sealed,
25   that no one give lodging to Mio Cid Ruy Díaz,
       and that whosoever might give it to him know verily,
       that they would lose their possessions and also the eyes from their face,
       and even their bodies and their souls.
       The Christian people had great sorrow,
30   they hide from Mio Cid, for they dare not say anything to him.
       The Campeador headed for his lodgings,
       as he arrived at the door, he found it securely locked,

for fear of King Alfonso, for so they had agreed,
34   that if he did not break it by force, that no one open it for him.]

The one-clause-at-a-time constraint first identified in novel speech by Pawley and Syder seems to be in play in the passage above. The speaker moves the narration of an idea or an event forward clause by clause, which apparently is a reflection of a constantly shifting focus of consciousness, typically between one and two seconds long. These brief spurts of speech are a 'universal feature of people's talk' (Chafe 1996, 40). Chafe has noted that it is not unusual for intonation units to consist of less than a clause and identifies noun phrases as especially common exceptions (41). In the passage from the *Cid*, noun phrases are also treated as single hemistichs, as in verses 15 (Mio Çid Ruy Díaz), 16 (sessaenta pendones), 16b (mugieres e varones), 17 (burgeses e burgesas), 22 (el rey don Alfonso), and 31 (El Campeador). Not clauses in a grammatical sense, they nonetheless represent an idea in the consciousness of the speaker, and this observation led Chafe to his one-new-idea hypothesis, essentially that a single intonation unit can express no more than one new idea (42).

While we may think of a term like 'constraint' as something that limits, this passage is considered genuinely expressive and poetic. The brief spurts of speech, in conjunction with the binary nature of the verse form, the use of assonance, and the formulaic expressions, are thought to have been pleasing to the audiences of the time and continue to satisfy readers today. The pleasure we derive from it may in fact be linked to the same cognitive constraints that are at work in its production. Intonation units represent the amount of information that can be active in the consciousness of the speaker at one time. They most likely also represent the optimal amount of information that can be processed by an audience of listeners.

In addition to understanding hemistichs as a cognitively constrained speech unit, the use of assonance in oral poetry, while aesthetically pleasing to us today, actually performs a constraining function. David C. Rubin, a cognitive psychologist whose work focuses on memory, has found that rhyme is a constraint used in oral composition as an aid to memorization. Rubin cites a number of studies that show how endrhyme facilitates recall, and is especially helpful in recalling the order of verses. In the experiments he cites, rhyme cues work best when they are similar but not identical to the ones used at learning (Rubin 1995, 83–4). Assonance, a fairly flexible form of rhyme, more flexible than perfect rhyme, may be especially suited to the needs of the poet of the Spanish epic, who may not be recalling verses verbatim but is most likely re-composing a narrative he has heard or has sung before. The small number of fixed formulas and the relative flexibility of assonance in the Spanish epic suggest a high degree of variability that is unlike the fixed phrases of the Homeric and Yugoslav poems. Later learned poetry in Spain increasingly exhibits the more demanding syllabic rhyme (matching tonic vowels and subsequent syllables) that we may think of as even more aesthetically pleasing. Novel rhyme, considered by moderns to signify good poetry, is probably only an option in written verse, since Rubin has found that in oral verse 'expected rhymes are more likely to be reproduced' than novel rhymes (85).

In the *Cid* the adjoining of hemistichs is carried out sequentially, which is a reflection in speech of the cognitive devices deployed in the processing of information. The narrator employs the simple paratactic syntax preferred by spontaneous speakers, with clause-final pauses evidenced throughout. Modern editors of the poem have traditionally identified the hemistichs as a kind of unit in the text by separating the same-verse hemistichs with a space or a space and a comma, and by placing at the end of each verse a comma or a period. These decisions are based on the syntax of the written poem, granting to each hemistich the status of a clause or phrase of one sort or another. Similarly, in the Pear Film narratives recorded by Chafe, the brief intonation units and the somewhat larger units display distinctive intonation contours and are transcribed as ending in commas and periods respectively. Chafe notes that even in unfamiliar languages a listener can detect every so often a falling intonation contour that we naturally associate with the end of a sentence. The change in intonation suggests that the speaker has determined that some kind of closure or completeness has been achieved. Sentence-final intonation generally coincides with what a grammarian would consider syntactic closure, essentially the completion of a sentence (Chafe 1980, 20). On average, sentence-final closure occurs after every three idea or intonation units (26). Exceptions do occur, such as narrating exclusively with single idea units and giving them sentence-final closure, and the production of fairly long narratives with only one or two sentence-final closures.

Although we can readily agree that the poet is narrating in hemistichs composed of one new idea at a time, it must be observed that these brief units also comprise much longer narrative segments. This suggests that we seem to be able to remember stories as wholes, while we focus on small pieces of these memories in recalling them. The entire memory can be narrated as a whole, or it can be produced in a series of brief intonation units (Chafe 1980, 26). Generally, however, in the narration of a story there are sequences of focuses of consciousness of an intermediate length that receive sentence-final intonation to signal their closure. It seems that as an organism we can best express a single focus of consciousness at a time, yet there is a need within us for more information than can be supplied by the limited capacity of a single focus of consciousness. When this need arises the information is scanned by a series of focuses of consciousness in order to comprehend and act upon it. The same process occurs when the information is relayed: a speaker deploys the focuses of consciousness sequentially until communication of the whole is complete. Chafe refers to the deployment of such a sequence of focuses of consciousness as a 'center of interest,' and the data from the Pear Film stories indicate that these sequences 'convey a single mental image about which several things are simultaneously true' (27). When the speaker determines that adequate communication of an image has been achieved, sentence-final intonation is employed.

Chafe assumes that the information-processing capabilities of the human organism lag behind its needs, which is why speakers do not express a series of centres of interest without some difficulty, which Chafe calls 'perturbations.' He divides these perturbations into five categories: 1) abandonment; 2) postponement; 3) pursuit of a side interest, with subsequent return to the main track; 4) insertion of a centre of interest on a different level of interest; and 5) supplementation of a centre of interest after preliminary closure has been reached (Chafe 1980, 33). As speakers switch from one centre of interest to another these perturbations are generally accompanied by corrections, pauses, repetitions, false starts, backtracking, and other manifestations of uncertainty in their speech. Although the 'niña de nuef años' episode cited earlier seems sequential, it actually alternates between what might be called background and foreground narration. By identifying these two spheres of narration in a single episode, we should be able to determine if its relative complexity has resulted in anything similar to Chafe's perturbations. A positive finding would provide supporting evidence of the oral composition of the passage, with its cognitive basis in speech.

The episode begins with an initial 'centre of interest,' or foreground action, the entrance of the Cid into Burgos and his reception by the residents, who are grieving over the Cid's predicament (vv. 15–20). From this initial centre of interest, the narrator then switches to a 'side interest,' or background action (vv. 21–8). Here the narrator explains the despair of the citizens of Burgos, already described as grieving, as a consequence of the prohibition by the king against aiding the Cid. The narration of the main action of the passage resumes (vv. 29–32), but the narrator again interrupts the flow of action to pursue another side interest (vv. 33–4), this time to explain why the door to the Cid's customary lodging was not opened.

The paratactic structure of the poem gives little sense of the scanning of centres of interest by the narrator. This may be a consequence of presenting the protagonist in action and the circumstances in which he acts without the use of subordinating conjunctions. The narrator presents first the foreground action, followed by some background information as explanation, then he returns to the main action and so forth. This narrative process produces something akin to the third of Chafe's five categories of perturbations: pursuit of a side interest with subsequent return to the main track. What Chafe found in his samples of spontaneous speech is that when the narrator returns to the main image, it is 'reverbalized' before the narration resumes (Chafe 1980, 34–5). This occurs in the passage from the *Cid*, where lines 18–20 are reverbalized in lines 29–30, as the narrator's focus returns to the initial centre of interest after he explains the reasons why the people of Burgos turned their backs on the Cid (lines 21–8).

Beginning at line 35 the narrator returns to the original centre of interest and presents the remainder of the Cid's encounter with the people of Burgos:

35   Los de Mio Çid   a altas vozes llaman,
        los de dentro   non les querién tornar palabra.
        Aguijó Mio Çid,   a la puerta se llegava,
        sacó el pie del estribera,   una ferídal' dava,
        non se abre la puerta,   ca bien era çerrada.
40   Una niña de nuef años   a ojo se parava,
        –Ya Campeador,   en buen ora çinxiestes espada,
        el rey lo ha vedado,   anoch d'él entró su carta
        con grant recabdo   e fuertemientre sellada.
        Non vos osariemos   abrir nin coger por nada,
45   si non, perderiemos   los averes e las casas
        e demás   los ojos de las caras.
        Çid, en el nuestro mal   vós non ganades nada,

mas el Criador vos vala   con todas sus vertudes santas.–
Esto la niña dixo   e tornós' pora su casa.
50   Ya lo vee el Çid,   que del rey non avié graçia,
51   partiós' de la puerta,   por Burgos aguijava, (*Cid*, vv. 35–51)

[35   The Cid's men call out loudly,
       those within would not respond.
       Mio Cid rode up, he came to the door,
       he drew his foot from the stirrup, he gave it a kick,
       the door doesn't open, for it was heavily secured.
40   A girl of nine years came into view,
       'Oh Campeador, in a fortunate hour you girded sword,
       the king has forbidden it, last night his letter arrived
       with much precaution and heavily sealed.
       We dare not open up or take you in for anything,
45   or else, we would lose our possessions and our houses
       and even the eyes from our faces.
       Cid, in our suffering you gain nothing,
       but may God help you with all his holy powers.'
       This the girl said and returned to her house.
50   Now the Cid sees it, that he had not the king's favour,
51   he moved away from the door, he spurred through Burgos]

The girl is a poetic device through whom the people of Burgos finally speak to the Cid. In rapid succession she conveys their admiration for him (v. 41), the king's prohibition (vv. 42–3), their current dilemma (vv. 44–6), a subtle plea for mercy (v. 47), and an expression of their hope for his future success (v. 48). Once she has greeted him (v. 41), the statements are narrated in a sequence of past, present, and future. Paratactic verse seems particularly well suited to the narration of events in this fashion. The focus is intense and the narration moves forward effectively. Although the girl does recapitulate verses 23–8 (vv. 42–6), here the information is communicated directly to the Cid, who can then understand why his customary lodgings are closed to him. Her speech has a pleasing aesthetic effect and exemplifies the skilled speaking that characterizes the verbal exchanges in the poem (Montgomery 1998, 98–100). In this passage the poet seems to be concentrating his cognitive energies on producing a speech that is memorable and powerfully persuasive, nothing at all like the speech of a nine-year-old child.

The principle of performance-enhanced speech may recall a similar concept in classical rhetorical prose, especially in the way it is subservient to natural constraints. In the case of oral delivery, the natural constraint is the need for the speaker to pause for breath. Breath pauses during performance result in short units of expression, identified and labelled by Cicero and Quintilian as essentially smaller parts of a whole. These are the 'limbs' of a 'body,' connected by 'joints,' which we recognize as the clauses of a sentence or period joined by conjunctions. The clause can be rhythmically complete but semantically meaningless, *membrum*, or both semantically and rhythmically incomplete, *incisun* or *articula* (Bakker 1997, 138–46).

Both classical rhetorical prose and epic verse are understood as constrained by nature in a fundamental way. In recognition of these constraints, the classical rhetors adapt their public speeches so as to create a pleasant and memorable experience for orator and audience alike. This experience is enhanced by the manipulation of breath units in a way that blends their syntax and rhythm of delivery, for audiences respond best to speech governed by nature. But the units of Latin rhetorical discourse, *membra*, are ultimately subservient to syntactic periodicity, in that 'they either create syntactic expectations or give "what is due" in fulfilling them' (Bakker 1997, 145). Epic discourse looks ahead as well, but not to the completion of a sentence or grammatical construct. Instead it projects toward the completion of the verse, to the simple assonance that marks the end of one verse and the beginning of another.

As the passage from the *Cid* confirms, a speaker does not process information quickly enough to be able to subordinate different centres of interest. Consequently, these are adjoined sequentially, as in parataxis, or in some cases coordinated with conjunctions, mostly *and*, less often *then*, *but*, or *so*. Speakers seldom use subordination, which leads to confusion (Chafe 1980, 30). As writers, we are familiar with the struggle to subordinate ideas and images into coherent prose. But this process of integration was not evidenced in the speech of Chafe's subjects in the late seventies, and neither is it found in the epic narratives of thirteenth-century Spain. The use of parataxis as a marker of speech, and of subordination as a marker of written discourse, can be exemplified in the prosification of the *Cid* passage in Alfonso X's *Estoria de España*, also from the thirteenth century (ca 1289). Subordinating conjunctions have been underlined:

Et pues que entró en Burgos fuesse pora la posada do solié posar; mas non le quisieron y acoger; ca el rey lo enuiara defender quel non acogiessen en ninguna posada en toda la uilla, nin le diessen uianda ninguna. Quando aquello uio el Çid, saliosse de la uilla et fue posar en la glera. (Menéndez Pidal 1906, 523 [chap. 851, 2nd column, lines 27–34]).

[And once he entered Burgos he went to the inn where he normally stayed, but they did not want to take him in there; for the king had ordered it prohibited that anyone should offer him lodging at any inn in all the town, or that they give him any provisions whatsoever. When the Cid saw that, he left the town and went to camp on the riverbank.]

Most striking is the absence from this passage of the moving encounter with the nine-year-old girl. Her breaking of the enforced silence implies solidarity between the Cid and the people of Burgos that the Alfonsine chroniclers could not abide.[5] With her removal, the tension disappears from the passage altogether. The use of subordinating conjunctions integrates the various centres of interest into a briefer yet syntactically more complex single focus. The process of transforming oral verse into prose produced the equivalent of a modern-day paragraph, with none of the repetition of the poem. Along with the repetitions, the different points of view are lost, resulting in the single point of view of the omniscient chronicler. The punctuation, determined by its modern editor Menéndez Pidal, now seems essential to it and underscores its literate essence (Fleischmann 1990b, 186–8).

Another aspect of the passage from the *Cid* that has been linked to its oral composition is evidenced in its use of what has been termed 'double narration.' John Gornall pointed out that if the *Cid* passage is 'taken consecutively, the Cid rode up to the door, retreated baffled, rode up to it again, and presumably losing his temper kicked it' (Gornall 2005, 105). Gornall considers more probable that the Cid 'approached the door once only, the shouts and the kick were simultaneous; and it was the combination of actions that produced the *niña*' (105). Gornall cites the verbal repetition (lines 32 and 37–9) and the more dignified scenario of a kick delivered at the outset as a sign of authority and not, as others would have it, of temper. Gornall goes on to cite seven more instances of double narration in the *Cid* and concludes that 'oral composition surely has a role to play in the presence of double narration both in the *chansons de geste* and the *PMC* [*Cid*] and its absence from modern written narratives' (114).

Gornall had identified instances of double narration in an earlier article but attributed their presence to a technique employed by the poet to emphasize important events in the narrative 'deliberately and appropriately' (Gornall 1987, 74). His conclusion is made in reference to Deyermond's identification of six important actions in the poem (three actions and three turning points in the action), which are meant to show ironic contrast as an artistic aim of the poet, 'carried out with great skill and striking success' (Deyermond 1973, 71). But Gornall notes that the poet does not employ double narration in all of Deyermond's six actions, and also uses the technique in comparatively unimportant contexts. This observation led Gornall to conclude that the poet used double narration to emphasize significant events in the poem, and at random. Its use can be seen as evidence of artistic coherence, or, and here he presages his final article on the subject by citing the findings of Jean Rychner on the *chansons de geste*, 'la reprise d'un thème menant à des variations sur ce thème' means we are in 'plein style oral' (Rychner 1955, 85, quoted in Gornall 1987, 75).

Rychner's reference to an oral style is not to be confused with oral composition, but to a style employed to facilitate memorization and later oral recitation by the jongleur (Rychner 1955, 85), much like the assumptions of Menéndez Pidal. Gornall's final judgment goes far beyond the concept of an oral style, as he concludes that the double narration found in the *Cid* must have involved oral composition. Gornall was not able to explore the issue any further, but he did provide a clear route for others to profit from his sharp analytical skills and insight. Following his lead, and adding to his analysis by employing the findings of Chafe and other linguists in the analysis of double narration in the *Cid*, we should achieve a more nuanced understanding of this unique characteristic of epic verse, and with it a more conclusive finding on its oral composition.

In both his earlier article and in its reprise, Gornall analyses examples of double narration in the episode in which the *Cid* hero humiliates the haughty Count of Barcelona (vv. 1017–36). The description and citations of the episode are the same as those used by Gornall in his later article, including the bold lettering (Gornall 2005, 108–10).[6]

The Cid's men prepare a banquet to celebrate their defeat of the Count of Barcelona. The Count contemptuously refuses to eat, declaring that he would rather die first:

A Mio Çid don Rodrigo grant cozina l'adobavan,
el conde don Remont non ge lo preçia nada,
adúzenle los comeres, delant ge los paravan,

él non lo quiere comer, a todos los sosañava:
'**Non combré un bocado, por quanto ha en toda España,**
antes perderé el cuerpo e dexaré el alma,
pues que tales malcalçados me vençieron de batalla.'

[For Mio Cid don Rodrigo they prepared a great banquet,
Count don Remont [he] does not appreciate it one bit,
they bring him the dishes, they put them before him,
he does not want to eat, he scorned them all:
'**I will not eat one mouthful, for anything in all of Spain,**
I will first lose my body and I will leave my soul,
now that such poorly shod men defeated me in battle'.]

In laisse 60 the Cid offers the Count his freedom if he will only eat:

Mio Çid Ruy Díaz odredes lo que dixo:
'**Comed, conde, d'este pan e beved d'este vino;**
si lo que digo fiziéredes, saldredes de cativo,
si non, en todos vuestros días non veredes christianismo.'

[**Mio Cid Ruy Diaz you will hear what he said:**
'**Eat, Count, of this bread and drink of this wine;**
if you were to do as I say, you will leave captivity,
if not, in all your days you will not see Christiandom.']

In laisse 61 the Count repeats his refusal to eat, persisting in it for three days:

Dixo el conde don Remont:
'Comede, don Rodrigo e pensedes de folgar,
que yo dexar me é morir, que non quiero comer.'
Fasta terçer día nol' pueden acordar;
ellos partiendo estas gananças grandes,
nol' pueden fazer comer un muesso de pan.

[Said Count don Remont:
'Eat, don Rodrigo, and feel free to relax,
for I·shall let myself die, for I do not wish to eat.'
Until the third day they cannot get him to agree;
they were dividing up these great riches,
they cannot get him to eat a single morsel of bread.]

Laisse 62, below, includes an offer by the Cid similar to that of laisse 60, with the additional promise of the release of two of the Count's knights.

> **Dixo Mio Çid: 'Comed, Conde, algo,**
> **ca si non comedes non veredes christianos;**
> e si vós comiéredes dón yo sea pagado,
> a vós e [a] dos fijos d'algo
> quitar vos he los cuerpos e dar vos é de mano.'

> [**Said Mio Cid: 'Eat, Count, something,**
> **for if you do not eat you will not see Christians**;
> and if you were to eat such that I be pleased,
> to you and to two nobles
> I will free your bodies and let you go.']

This is followed by a final line (v. 1036), which Gornall sees as 'pointing to double narration' in the dialogue (Gornall 2005, 109):

> Quando esto oyó el conde, yas' iva **alegrando**.
> [When the Count heard this, now he started to cheer up.]

As Gornall notes, when the passage is read consecutively, laisse 60 is understood as mere encouragement, freedom not being offered until laisse 62 – that is, unless the freedom of his knights is more important than his own, which would then account for his happiness only in line 1036. If double narration is taken into account, the Cid's offer in line 1026 (saldredes de cativo) is an offer of freedom. The refusal of laisse 61 is not a response to laisse 60, but a second narration of the refusal of laisse 59. Likewise, the offer of freedom in laisse 62 is not new – it is a second narration of laisse 60 – while the inclusion of the Count's knights in laisse 62 is elaboration. Gornall also points out that the 'strophic patterning,' meaning the change in assonance, does not mark the double narration, but instead marks the change in speakers. The Count's happiness should be understood as a reaction to the offer expressed twice, in laisses 60 and 62, but made only once by the Cid on the third day and accepted immediately by the starving Count.

By acknowledging the use of double narration in the passage, Gornall is able to correct critical misreadings that saw two offers made by the Cid to the Count. According to these readings the Cid's position softens as he is confronted with a defiant and starving Count, and he is thought to have sweetened his initial offer of release by agreeing to free two nobles as well as the Count (Gornall 1987, 72). Gornall insists that the Cid's offer did not change when he was faced with the Count's resistance. Rather, he made the offer only once, on the third day, when the starving Count would not refuse him, in spite of the humiliation he would have to undergo (Gornall 2005, 110). This interpretation is simpler and more in tune with the representation of the Cid in the rest of the poem than previous explanations. Gornall also concludes that this and the seven other examples of double narration he studies are evidence that oral composition played a role in the production of the poem (114).

Although Gornall's findings lend support to the thesis being presented here, his conclusion would benefit from additional support. This may be found in the link that Gornall identifies between strophic patterning and a change in speakers; in other words, a change in the end-line assonance parallels a change in speaker. This observation accords with the findings of Bayo on the poem in general, in which the term 'deitic dissonance' is offered in reference to 'the contrast produced between the endings of two successive verse lines that do not enter in a rhyme relationship, and whose function is to point out a narrative transition' (Bayo 2001, 86–7). Examples of these transitions include 'the beginning of a new narrative sequence, a change of focus, the switch between narration and direct speech, a change of speaker to hearer, the inner articulation of a character's discourse, and non-sequential storytelling' (87). Bayo stresses the autonomy of this 'traditional technique in Old Spanish heroic poetry' (Bayo 90), from the French *Chanson de geste*, and suggests that the numerous couplets and unrhymed verses [*versos sueltos*] of the *Cid* should not be considered copyist errors but an essential part of the poet's art.

The findings by Gornall and Bayo find further substantiation in Chafe's analysis of spoken discourse, most notably in the difficulties experienced by speakers as they move from one centre of interest to another. One way in which Chafe was able to measure the degree of difficulty experienced was by counting in seconds the hesitation involved in reorienting the narrative. The amount of hesitation varies, but generally it is less between the idea units within a centre of interest than between idea units across 'a sentence boundary,' the boundary between two centres of interest (Chafe 1980, 43). From his examination of the kinds of transitions in content between these boundaries and the amount of hesitation involved, Chafe concluded that the degree of difficulty in moving from one centre of interest to another increases with the amount of reorientation required. Of course hesitation by medieval minstrels is not recorded in manuscript texts, but Bayo's concept of deitic dissonance and its connection to narrative transitions seems to correlate well with Chafe's findings regarding hesitation in spontaneous spoken narrative and gives us reason enough to undertake a fuller analysis of the episode of the Count of Barcelona.

In this episode, changes in assonance do occur in moments of transition in the narrative, as Gornall notes, and very much like others that Bayo indicates and attributes to poetic technique. But this attribution to poetic technique is at best only partially true, because it does not explain the existence of other instances of transition in the narrative in which no change in assonance occurs, a number of which can be found in the latter portion of the same episode (vv. 1033–76). Chafe's observation that transitions between centres of interest may occur with more or less hesitation, depending on the amount of difficulty involved in the reorientation, suggests another way to understand the narrative transitions in the *Cid* and to distinguish between those accompanied by changes in assonance and those that are not.

The perturbations in the narrative flow of the speech of Chafe's subjects are indicators of the difficulty they experienced in moving from one centre of interest to another. Chafe categorized these perturbations as 1) abandonment; 2) postponement; 3) pursuit of a side interest with subsequent return to the main track; 4) insertion of a centre of interest on a different level of interest; and 5) supplementation of a centre of interest after preliminary closure has been reached. The category of postponement may best describe the cognitive process that led to the repetition of the offer of freedom by the Cid to the Count of Barcelona. In this process the speaker starts off with a particular sequence of focuses in mind, only to realize that something else should be verbalized first, and finally returns to the initial focus (Chafe 1980, 33–4). Another look at the episode, this time with the aid of Chafe's concepts of narrative development, should help identify the cognitive processes involved.

The first centre of interest is identifiable as the presentation of the scene outside the Cid's tent, described a few lines earlier in the poem:

De fuera de la tienda un salto dava,
de todas partes los sos se ayuntavan,
plogo a Mio Çid, ca grandes son las gananças. (vv. 1014–16)

[Outside the tent he [Mio Cid] made a leap,
from all parts his men came together,
it pleased Mio Cid, for great are the spoils.]

The introduction of a setting is typical in the narration of specific episodes as it satisfies the need to orient the listener of the story. The speaker may reactivate the setting, also termed 'orientation' by Chafe, with minimal difficulty (Chafe 1994, 128).

The next centre of interest is the preparation of the banquet, followed by the Count's reaction to it, which is first narrated and then spoken by the Count himself. The food is delivered to the same setting just described, so there is little disruption in the narration. The two protagonists of the episode have been introduced previously and continue to be involved here. What is new information is the preparation of the food and the Count's response to it and to his hosts, whom he despises:

A Mio Çid don Rodrigo grant cozina l'adobavan,
el conde don Remont non ge lo preçia nada,
adúzenle los comeres, delant ge los paravan,
él non lo quiere comer, a todos los sosañava:
'Non combré un bocado por quanto ha en toda España,
antes perderé el cuerpo e dexaré el alma,
pues que tales malcalçados me vençieron de batalla.' (vv. 1017–23)[7]

The Count does not seem to be speaking to the Cid or his men directly, since he refers to them with derision and in third person (me vençieron; 'they defeated me'). He is most likely speaking to himself. His derision of the Castilians and their banquet offering sets the stage for the standoff with the Cid.

The narrator then introduces the response of the Cid to the Count's refusal, which includes an offer of freedom for the Count if he agrees to partake of the banquet offering, and a warning that if he does not agree, he will never be set free:

Mio Çid Ruy Díaz, odredes lo que dixo:
'Comed, conde, d'este pan e beved d'este vino,
si lo que digo fiziéredes, saldredes de cativo,
si non, en todos vuestros días non veredes christianismo.' (vv. 1024–7)

This passage seems to form one centre of interest, the verbal equivalent of an image being scanned in the mind of the speaker, who then communicates the full image through a series of idea units.

The response of the Count is unaffected by the offer of freedom, and this next centre of interest is little more than a repetition of the Count's initial derisive reaction to the first banquet offering, but this time he speaks directly to the Cid:

> Dixo el conde don Remont,
> 'Comede, don Rodrigo e pensedes de folgar,
> **que yo dexar me é morir, que non quiero comer.'** (vv. 1028–30)[8]

The narration of the episode seems to have stalled during the articulation of this centre of interest. An indication that something may be amiss is the lapse in the assonance, as 'Dixo el conde don Remont' does not rhyme with the line before or after – christianismo / Remont / folgar – nor does 'comer,' which editors like to change to 'yantar' to rhyme it with 'acordar' in the following verse (Montaner 1993, 162). But in following our division into centres of interest, it seems rather clear that 'que non quiero comer' is the final intonation or idea unit in the articulation of the centre of interest that constitutes the Count's response to the Cid's offer of freedom and is not connected to the next line in the episode, which is part of the ensuing centre of interest. This leaves a three-line centre of interest with no rhyme, which suggests that the narrator has lost focus or, in Chafe's terminology, there may be too much stress on the cognitive capabilities of the narrator to express what is in his short-term memory and to develop the narrative.

In the Pear Film stories there are instances in which a centre of interest may be cognitively unified but at the same time shows signs of syntactic and intonational uncertainty, Chafe's perturbations. In the category of postponement, a speaker begins to express a centre of interest in a certain way, only to decide that something needs to be added. The speaker suspends the narrative progression, adds what is missing, and then returns to repeat the initial focus (Chafe 1980, 33–4). In such cases the one-to-one correspondence between a centre of interest and an intonationally defined sentence is disturbed. The irregularity in the assonance of the passage above most likely signals a similar perturbation in the sequencing in the narration of centres of interest. As the narrator gives the Count's response to the Cid's offer, he realizes that he has left out an important detail, the three-day duration of the Count's refusal:

> Fasta terçer día nol' pueden acordar;
> ellos partiendo estas gananças grandes,
> nol' pueden fazer comer un muesso de pan. (vv. 1030–2)

This centre of interest returns us to the original setting. Here the Cid and his men are counting their booty, enjoying their banquet, and have delivered the banquet food to the Count with the expectation that he too will join in the celebration of his defeat. The Cid has yet to speak to him.

Now that the missing three-day fast has been added, the poet repeats the narration of the offer of freedom to the Count, here with more detail than before:

> Dixo Mio Çid, 'Comed, Conde, algo,
> ca si non comedes, non veredes christianos,
> e si vós comiéredes, dón yo sea pagado,
> a vós e dos fijos d'algo
> quitar vos he los cuerpos e dar vos é de mano.' (vv. 1033–5b)

The response of the Count is joy, which after three days of hunger strike seems most appropriate:

> Quando esto oyó el conde, yas' iva **alegrando** (v. 1036)

His hunger will compel him to eat with the gusto the Cid is demanding and so heighten his humiliation before the Castilians. As Gornall points out, the Cid knew exactly when to intervene, which was only once (Gornall 1987, 74).

The examination of the passage through the lens of Chafe's findings on spontaneous speech yields some surprising results. Specialists have generally accepted that the Cid made his offer only once, ascribing the repetition of the offer to poetic technique (Montaner 1993, 162, note to v. 1028). The repetition of the offer of freedom to the Count turns out not to be a poetic technique at all, whether we think of technique in terms of an artist emphasizing what is important, as Gornall originally thought, or as a way to highlight transitions in the narration, as Bayo asserts. The repetition is better understood as a manifestation of the difficulty of managing the various centres of interest that constitute the narration of this confrontation. The poet is engaging his focus of consciousness, or short-term memory, in the production of brief idea units, placing one after another in the adding-on syntax preferred in spontaneous oral discourse, while signalling the end of each line through genre-specific assonance. At the same time the poet is engaging another level of consciousness in the movement from one centre of interest to another. It is precisely at this moment of movement to another centre of interest that the heightened demand on the cognitive capabilities of a narrator tends to produce a perturbation in the flow of the narrative. In this particular case, the poet seems to have moved on to the Cid's offer of freedom before he had explained that the Count had spent three days in hungry defiance. And so, soon after realizing his miscue, the poet stumbles a bit with the syntax and the assonance of the premature first response of the Count (Dixo el conde don Remont ...), and then returns to describe the Count's three-day resistance. Only then can he return to narrate the Cid's offer and the Count's joyous response. The remainder of the episode is narrated without additional perturbations, although a number of transitions are involved.

In order to fully accept the explanation offered for the repetitions and lapses in assonance of the passage, we need to explain as well the smooth narration of the remainder of the episode, lines 1037–76 – in other words, why some transitions are more difficult than others and what this tells us about the cognitive processes involved in the movement from one centre of interest to another. Chafe distinguishes between a more acute focus of consciousness, that of the short-term memory in the deployment of intonation units, and a peripheral consciousness that is aware of expectations for the development of a particular discourse topic. To explain the difference he invokes a parallel with vision, since both consciousness and vision have a focal component with high acuity and another of lesser acuity that serves to provide a context for the focus and to direct the focus to possible proximate focuses. Chafe presumes that the parallel between vision and consciousness is a reflection of the development of the processing of both perceived and remembered information in the eye and brain together (Chafe 1980, 40).

In this formulation, and continuing the analogy with vision, it is the function of our peripheral consciousness to direct our consciousness to its next perch. In this way a speaker is able to move from one centre of interest to another and to scan each centre of interest for the information that would satisfy the speaker and the listener. There would be more than one available perch for our consciousness, but its selection takes place while the speaker is communicating the more specific focuses of consciousness in speech. Chafe offers some general information that our peripheral consciousness requires for its orientation, such as place, time, people, their salient characteristics, background activity, and so forth (Chafe 1980, 42). By comparing the time of hesitation of speakers as they move from one centre of interest to another, presumably guided by their peripheral consciousness, Chafe was able to determine that the longest hesitations occur when a new orientation is required (44) – in other words, when additional background information must be given for the new perch to be established.

In the *Cid* narrative, the description of the three-day fast was skipped as the speaker moved forward to the description of the offer of freedom to the Count. When he became aware that he had omitted the Count's three-day fast, and could not plausibly portray the Count as accepting the offer of the Cid without having offered some resistance, he stumbled through the Count's response before returning to the background information required for the orientation of the episode. The evidence for the stumbling of the poet in the Count's first response lies in the irregular division of the hemistichs and the absence of assonance (vv. 1028–30). These poetic failings are equivalent to the extended hesitations and lack of coincidence between syntactic and intonational closure found in the Pear Film stories at moments of change in orientation. The reorientation that caused the most difficulty involved a temporal overlap – that is, a requirement to say something about one event while another was proceeding (Chafe 1980, 46). In the *Cid* passage this difficulty is compounded because the poet returns to a previous point in his narration to give additional background information after initiating the dialogue that is dependent upon it.

A final consideration must be given to the fact that the poet is not relating an event witnessed by him, but an event he has either created or heard narrated by another poet. At some level he is guided by the desire to tell a compelling story. If his peripheral consciousness is guiding him from one perch to another in the development of this story, then this development must follow some kind of narrative model. Here again we may look to recordings and analysis of spontaneous speech, in this case a series of dinner-table conversations in which Chafe identifies a 'discourse topic,' defined as a combination of a series of centres of interest that in the mind of the speaker form a coherent 'narrative' (Chafe 1994, 120–1, 127–8). The verbalization of these narratives follows a pattern that typically includes the following elements: 1) orientation, 2) complication, 3) climax, 4) denouement, and, finally, 5) coda. In Chafe's findings, the purpose of these conversational narratives is to tell something unexpected, treating 'the unexpected event as the climax of a set of ideas leading up to and away from it' (128).

The first two elements are readily observable in the episode between the Cid and the Count of Barcelona. Chafe's orientation can be understood as the initial setting, the Cid's camp and the defeated Count, surrounded by the Castilians dividing the spoils of their battlefield victory and preparing a victory feast. The complication is the refusal by the Count to accept the food offered by the Castilians, and the expressed determination to die rather than eat. After this would come the climax, which in Chafe's formulation is an unexpected event. The event that seems to correspond best to Chafe's definition is the Cid's offer of freedom to the Count in exchange for his participation in the banquet celebrating his own defeat. Chafe observes that the climax is 'usually presented with bells and whistles' and can be spread over a number of intonation units, with one intonation unit becoming the climax within the climax (Chafe 1994, 131–2). In the example he cites, the speaker is narrating an event she witnessed on a hiking trip in which an elderly couple was leading the way:

a)   And the two of them,
b)   got to the rise,
c)   and the next minute,
d)   they just fell over.
e)   Totally.
f)   I mean I guess the stop,
g)   was just too much,
h)   and they both of them just totally passed out.
i)   I mean (Chafe 1994, 130)[9]

The narrator delivers the climax a first time (a–d), with *d* being the climax within the climax. There follows a brief reinforcement (one intonation unit: 'totally'), then an attempt at explanation, and finally further reinforcement through repetition with different wording (h). Like Chafe's narrator, the narrator of the *Cid* reiterates his climax, in this case the offer of freedom to the Count (vv. 1024–7 and 1033–5b). And in both cases, after the first iteration of the climax, there is an attempt to explain how it came about, in effect an emphasis on the unexpectedness of the event, before the narrator repeats it (*Cid*: vv. 1030–2, Chafe: f–g).

The remainder of the narration includes the denouement and the coda. In Chafe's formulation a denouement 'involves moves that will return consciousness to a new state of normality in which expectations have been adjusted to include the new and unexpected knowledge' (Chafe 1994, 131). In a spoken dialogue – that is, one between two or more interlocutors – it is common for the denouement to include an interactive sequence in which statements of surprise are expressed,

confirming for the speaker that 'the climactic event was indeed unexpected' and 'worth telling' (131). The audience reaction is not recorded in the poem, but the Count expresses joyful surprise at the Cid's
offer of freedom:

Cuando esto oyó el conde yas'iva alegrando,
'Si lo fiziéredes, Çid, lo que avedes fablado,
tanto cuanto yo viva seré dent maravillado.' (vv. 1036–8)

[When the Count heard this, now he started to cheer up,
'If you do this, Cid, what you have said,
for as long as I live I will be amazed by it.']

The denouement ends with a return to normality, in this case a statement by the Cid that the Count can expect no more special treatment,
but a return to pillaging as warranted by circumstances (lines 1041–8).
The coda, described by Chafe as a meta-comment on the narrated
events, occurs after the Count's release, as he keeps turning back to
look at the Cid (lines 1076–81). He cannot bring himself to believe that
the Cid will keep his promise of freedom and fears he will go back on
his word. In his meta-commentary on the narrated events, the poet affirms the Cid would never commit such a disloyal act and that in fact
he never did:

lo que non ferié el caboso por cuanto en el mundo ha,
una deslealtança, ca non la fizo alguandre' (vv. 1080–1)

[which the worthy one would not do for anything in the world,
a disloyal act, for he never did it.]

The double narration of the Conde de Barcelona episode has been
explained here in two ways. In the first formulation the repetition of the
Cid's offer of freedom is a function of cognitive constraints experienced
by the poet as he simultaneously narrates the episode and looks ahead
to its satisfactory conclusion. In looking forward, an important detail is
left out, so the poet returns to the event in order to restore the missing
detail and relate the episode coherently. In the second formulation, the
repetition is meant to emphasize the climax in the narration of an unexpected event. Yet, the narrative model employed is universal, as opposed to the artistic aim of an individual poet. It is, however, artful in

the sense that it ensures that the event does cause surprise, which makes it worth telling. In either formulation, the double narration occurs because the events are being narrated orally, without recourse to writing.

The parallels between the cognitive characteristics of the spontaneous speech of Chafe's subjects and the expression of the Cid narrative are striking. Chafe's analysis of recorded speech allowed him to identify the cognitive processes involved in the narration of the events portrayed in the Pear Film and of other events brought up in casual conversation as stories worth telling. His examples are all from late twentieth-century America. The *Cid* is a vernacular epic narrative put to parchment in the kingdom of Castile in 1207, yet it seems to show cognitive processes and organization of discourse topics similar to those of Chafe's subjects. The Spanish epic follows conventions specific to a medieval narrative genre and a culture very distant from twentieth-century America, which makes the similarities between them even more striking. Their similarities most likely stem from the fact that they are being produced before an audience, with decisions about expression, emphasis, and effectiveness being made in real time.

In the next chapter the methodology deployed here will be used to gain insight into the compositional mode of the *Poema de Fernán González*. The poem celebrates the life of Fernán González, a Castilian warrior who lived in the first half of the tenth century. His legendary accomplishments inspired a thirteenth-century cleric from the Castilian monastery of San Pedro de Arlanza to compose a narrative of his deeds in the learned verse form known as *cuaderna vía*.

4 The *Poema de Fernán González*

The *Poema de Fernán González* is exceptional in a number of ways. Like the *Cid*, the poem recreates the heroic deeds of a Castilian warrior, Count Fernán González. Also a historical personage, Fernán González waged war and politics aggressively in the mid-tenth century (Salvador Martínez 1991, 9–16; López Guil 2001, 123–8), and his legendary status rests on his relentless pursuit of the independence of Castile from the kingdom of León. In much the same way that the historical Cid and the poem are connected to the Castilian monastery San Pedro de Cardeña, the Fernán González of history is linked to the monastery of San Pedro de Arlanza (Salvador Martínez 1991, 16–17), and the poem that recounts his deeds most likely was put to parchment there between 1250 and 1252 (23). Unlike the *Cid*, the *Fernán González* is narrated in *cuaderna vía* (four-fold way), a learned verse form of four-line strophes of mono-rhymed alexandrine verse, and retains a notable ecclesiastical influence in its expression and subject matter (Bailey 1993). Because of its composition in a learned verse form, scholars have assumed that the poem was composed in writing. But as the previous chapters have made clear, oral composition played a primary role in learned texts as well as in vernacular epic poetry. The insights gained from the analysis and findings of the previous chapters will serve as a point of departure for the analysis of the role of oral composition in the *Fernán González*.

As an important political figure in tenth-century Spain, Fernán González is mentioned in a number of Latin texts, but the most extensive early reference is found in the *Chronica Naierensis*.[1] The chronicle includes a few episodes from the life of Fernán González, including the Christian victory over Abd al-Rahman III, the Muslim caliph of Cordoba (912–61), at the battle of Simancas on 6 August 938 (López-Guil 2001,

125). The battle also plays an increasingly important role in subsequent narratives depicting Fernán González and serves here as a touchstone for an examination of the way in each text the legendary battle is re-created with a distinct purpose and perspective. In all accounts of the battle an eclipse occurs and this is considered a sign from God, but only in the *Chronica* is this sign understood in political terms, with the focus directed on King Ramiro II of León (930–50). Fernán González is mentioned only in passing in the previous episode, and not at all in the battle of Simancas.

The Latin text tells us that [In the Era 971 [933 A.D.], King Ramiro staying in León, a message came from Fernán González that a large Muslim military expedition [*azeifa*] is moving quickly toward Castile. King Ramiro moves his army in order to meet the enemy in Osma 'Oxoma', and invoking the name of God, prepares for battle.] The continuation of the Latin text and its translation follow:

> Dedit illi Dominus uictoriam magnam: partim ex eis occidit, partim multa milia captiuorum secum adduxit et reuersus est ad propriam sedem cum uictoria magna (Estévez Sola 1995, 131)

> [God gave him a great victory: he killed some of them, some, many thousands of prisoners, he took with him and returned to his own residence with a great victory.][2]

There is no mention of Fernán González in the description of the battle of Simancas that follows, but it serves here as the starting point in a series of texts that portray the battle in divergent ways. The Latin text tells us that [Ramiro gathers his army and proceeds to Zaragoza 'Cesaraugustam'. The Saracen king Abholaia bowed his neck to the great king Ramiro and subjugated all the land to the dominion of our king. He deceived his king Abderramam of Córdoba and surrendered with all his men to the Catholic king. This our king, who as he was strong and powerful, conquered all the fortresses that were hostile to Abohaya and turned them over to him, and returned to León with a great victory.] The continuation of the Latin text and its translation follow:

> Abohayha iterum regem Ranimirum fefellit et ad Abderraamam pro pace misit. Et iterum uenerunt Sarraceni Cordubensis cum magno exercitu Septimancas properauit. Tunc ostendit Deus signum magnum in celo et

reuersus est sol in tenebras in uniuerso mundo por unam horam diei. Rex noster Catholicus hec audiens illuc ire disposuit cum magno exercitu et ibidem confligentibus ad inuicem dedit Dominus uictoriam regi Catholico feria IIII[a] imminente festo Sanctorum Iusti et Pastoris, era DCCCCLXXI[a]. Deleta sunt ex eis LXXX milia Maurorom; etiam ipse Abohaya rex Agarenorum ibidem a nostris comprehensus est et Legionem aduectus et ergastulo trusus. Et quia mentitus est domino Ranimiro comprehensus est recto iuditio Dei. Illi uero qui remanserunt itinere arrepto in fugan uersi sunt, rege uero illos persequente, et dum ipsi peruenerunt ad urbem qui dicitur Alhandega, a nostri ibidem comprehensi et extincti sunt. Ipse uero rex Abderrachmam semiuiuus euasir. Vnde nostri multa attulerunt spolia, aurum uidelicet et argentum et uestes preciosas. Rex quidem iam securus perrexit ad domun suam cum uictoria magna in pace deinde post duos dies. (Estévez Sola 1995, 131)

[Abohayha in turn deceived King Ramiro and sent to Abderraamam for peace. And in response the Saracens of Córdoba rushed to Simancas with a great army. Then God showed a great sign in the sky and the sun turned dark in all the world for one hour of the day. Our Catholic king hearing this set out to go there with a great army and in that very place combating each other God gave the victory to the Catholic king on Wednesday near the feast day of Saints Justus and Pastor [6 August], in the Era 971 [933 A.D.]. 80,000 Moors were wiped out by him; and this very Abohaya king of the Hagarenes in that same place was captured and was taken to León and forced into chains. And because he lied to Lord Ramiro he was dealt with in accordance with the right judgment of God. Those who remained took to the road in flight, and with the king in pursuit, until they came upon the city that is called Alhandega, in that place by us they were captured and killed. This king Adderrachmam escaped half alive. From where ours took great spoils, clearly gold and silver and precious garments. The king certainly proceeded safely to his home with a great victory in peace from there after two days.]

In this description of the event, then, God seems to respond to the treason of Abohaya through an eclipse of the sun and a battle ensues. Final judgment is passed in God's name on Abohaya, king of the Hagarenes, for his act of treason against a Christian king. Abd al-Rahman barely escapes with his life, and the Christians return in triumph with great spoils. God's will has been done, but the men do the fighting and reap the rewards of their actions. It is a thoroughly political reading of an important battle in the Christian struggle against the Moors, some 250 years after the fact.

This same battle serves as the basis for a privilege conceded by Fernán González in 934 to the Castilian monastery of San Millán de la Cogolla (Dutton 1967, 1–9). The document is included in the registry [*becerro*] of the monastery, which one would expect from such a foundational document, although by all accounts the document is fraudulent and actually dates from the early years of the thirteenth century (2). The text of the privilege describes four astronomical portents as occurring in the Spanish era 972 [934 A.D.], including the same darkening of the sun and the later weakening of its brightness described in the chronicle:

> In Era nonagentesima septuagesima secunda, xiiij kalendas agusti, lumen solis die viᵃ feria amittens lucendi virtutem obscuratum consitit ab hora secunda in terciam. Iiijᵃ feria idus octobris colorem eiusdem solis multi cognouerunt effectum pallidum. (Dutton 1967, 2)

> [In the Era 972, fourteen days before the first of August, on a Friday, the light of the sun losing its strength, became dark from the second to the third hour. On Wednesday 15 October again many recognized a pale effect on the colour of the sun.]

These portents are interpreted as an expression of God's anger at the Christian leaders for allowing the barbarians to dominate them. As Abd al-Rahman assembles his massive army, the Christians look to God for succour. King Ramiro promises to make gifts to the basilica of Santiago [Saint James], and Fernán González, inspired by his example, makes a similar promise to the monastery of San Millán de la Cogolla [Saint Emilianus], all in the hope that the saints will be pleased and help turn God to the Christian side. The saints and a celestial army of angels subsequently descend from Heaven and lead the Christians to victory.[3] Nothing is said about the outcome for Abd al-Rahman, although the Christians slaughter the Muslims and seize the book of their perdition, presumably the Koran, and the high priest or bishop who led them astray, as well as all their tents: 'Pluribusque de illis auersis gladijs cesis, librum sue perdicionis ac pontificem caput suj erroris cum omnibus tentorijs suis cepimus' (Dutton 1967, 3).[4] Because the saints and their army of angels turned the battle in favour of the Christians, the spoils go to the houses of Santiago and San Millán. The privilege then identifies the localities that must make perpetual payments to the monastery of San Millán for the aid rendered to the Christian forces, authorized by God, and under his authority, Count Fernán González of Castile, King García I Sánchez of Pamplona (Navarre), and King Ramiro II of León.

In a vernacular prose version of the privilege, transcribed in 1387, the portents are again described and are said to be a sign from Jesus Christ of his anger towards the Christian leaders for living in mortal sin by paying an annual tribute to the Muslim king of sixty young virgins ('mancebas en cabello'), thirty of noble birth and thirty peasants (Dutton 1967, 13).[5] Jesus was so moved by the cries and suffering of the girls that he sent a messenger to breathe into the hearts of the king and his counsellors the idea that it is better to die honourably then to live dishonourably, and to let God do with them as he pleases: 'Más uale buena muerte morir que beuir uida desonrada, mas faga Dios lo que quisiere de nos.' When the Muslims arrive to take charge of their tribute, they are beheaded, and the corrective action is soon set into motion. As the Christian leaders await in dread the attack of the Muslim army, the Holy Spirit enters the heart of King Ramiro and he is moved to declare Santiago king of his land, his body, and his people. King García Sánchez and Count Fernán González make the same declaration to San Millán, making him their king and lord. That night an angel visits them in their sleep and declares that as long as they promise not to forget the glorious act that God will perform on behalf of the two saints who are pleading to God for mercy, God will deliver them from their anxiety and danger: 'Sacaruos ha el Señor del Çielo de la coyta e del peligro en que uos estades' (Dutton 1967, 15). After the battle is won, and Abd al-Rahman captured and beheaded, the Christians turn joyous and declare that the two saints were their kings and leaders, all of which leads to the donation of one-fifth of the booty from the battle in equal amounts to San Millán and Santiago, and the promise of annual payments in perpetuity, along with the promise of eternal damnation for anyone who ignores the privilege.

The Latin privilege seems to be the basis for the recreation of the battle of Simancas in a *cuaderna vía* poem on the life of San Millán by Gonzalo de Berceo, *La vida de San Millán de la Cogollla* (ca 1234). Berceo wrote a number of narrative poems, but this one honours the patron of the monastery where Berceo lived and worked, the same monastery that produced the Latin privilege. The passage dedicated to the battle is extensive (stanzas 366–481) and, like the Latin privilege, clearly binds King Ramiro to the promise made to Santiago, and Fernán González to the promise made to San Millán (stanzas 426–32). Berceo adds dramatic touches to the story, such as dialogue and his own comments on the events he narrates. More importantly, Berceo brings the story to life for his audience, saying that if they had made the payments as prescribed, then the hard times they are experiencing could have been avoided, and if they renew the payments, the good times will return (stanzas 479–80).

Judging solely by the reference to the solar eclipse, Berceo seems to follow the Latin privilege (stanzas 378–9), although the date is different for the second portent, the waning of the sun's brightness, occurring here in early September instead of mid-October:

> Desend en el setiembre, luego en la entrada,
> miérco[r]es es a meydía murió otra vegada;
> tornó plus amariello qe la cera colada,
> ante qe revisclas[s]e fue grant ora passada (stanza 380)

> [And then in September, at the very beginning,
> on a Wednesday at midday it died again;
> it turned more pale than poured wax,
> before it revived a long time had passed.]

He then versifies the first few entries from the list of the many towns and villages that are indebted to San Millán for their deliverance from the Muslim menace. In doing so Berceo follows the entries of the Latin privilege nearly verbatim (stanzas 468–74), until skipping a few of the towns and then admitting that the names are difficult, hard to match, and cannot all be fit into the rhyme scheme. He then states that he prefers to tell the story plainly (without all the details):

> Los nomnes son revueltos, graves de acordar,
> no los podemos todos en rimas acoplar;
> más vos quiero la cosa planamientre contar
> qe prender grand trabajo e el corso damnar (vv. 475c–d)

> [The names are difficult, hard to match,
> we cannot turn them all into rhymed verse;
> I prefer to tell the thing plainly
> than to take on a huge task and spoil the metre.]

Berceo's *San Millán* incorporates minute details of the Latin text, although the date of the second portent differs. Another discrepancy occurs as Berceo reminds his audience that he is taking details from a written text, then gives the place of the battle as Campo de Toro, whereas in the Latin privilege the place of the battle is not identified:

> Qui saberlo quisiere, esto bien lo entienda,
> ca assí lo leemos e dizlo la leyenda,
> en el Campo de Toro cuntió esta fazienda,
> y prisieron christianos de moros tal emienda. (stanza 456)

> [Whoever would like to know it, should understand this well,
> for we read it and the written text tells it thus,
> in Campo de Toro occurred this event,
> there Christians took from the Moors this remedy.]

On the one hand Berceo follows the Latin privilege closely, yet there are other instances when important details do not match. This may mean that Berceo is not following the same privilege that has been preserved for us, or, as occurs in other instances, the author may be basing his poem on a written text but feels no compunction to follow it verbatim.[6]

When the episode of the battle is recreated in the *Fernán González*, it takes on new meaning and in the process has been transformed, with important differences in every detail. The battle becomes the battle of Hacinas, and Fernán González fights the Muslim general Almanzor (stanzas 377–558). The episode is no longer at the service of a privilege but is one in a series of episodes in a narrative designed to highlight the deeds of Fernán González, count and liberator of Castile, albeit with a debt to San Millán and Santiago, as in the privilege, but with an even stronger link to San Pelayo, a monk from the monastery of San Pedro de Arlanza. The monastery was supported in life by the historical Fernán González, and in death it was the site of the entombment of his mortal remains and of the composition of the poem.

Other episodes in the poem show parallels with previous written texts, both direct and indirect (López-Guil 2001, 49–75). It is also likely that its composition involved the adaptation of an undocumented epic poem on Fernán González. Probably the best insight into the tenor and expression of that poem can be found in the episodes from his life succinctly narrated in the *Mocedades de Rodrigo*, amid the legendary deeds of the early Castilian ancestors of the Cid and King Fernando I (Bailey 2007, vv. 31–105). These same episodes live on in the Spanish ballads of the sixteenth century, which in turn inspired a seventeenth-century play by Lope de Vega, *El Conde Fernán González*. The thirteenth-century Alfonsine *Estoria de España* incorporates the *Fernán González* into its vernacular prose history of Spain, although in this version the rebellious count is purposefully transformed into a colourless and submissive vassal of the king of León, the very antithesis of his heroic projection in the poem, yet a good example of Alfonso projecting his own vision of kingship through historical texts (Bailey 1996).

These examples help us appreciate how the composition of texts recounting the deeds of a legendary figure such as Fernán González served the ends of the institutions that sponsored their placement onto parchment. In the case of the *Fernán González*, we should also understand that the poem was part of a genre of Spanish vernacular poetry that emerged in the thirteenth century, known as *mester de clerecía* (the cleric's craft). The term emphasizes the fact that it was the preferred mode of expression of learned authors who composed poems on a variety of subjects, including the Virgin Mary, most especially the recounting of miracles performed by her; the lives and deeds of local saints; as well as the epic deeds of subjects from late antiquity such as Alexander of Macedonia and Apollonius of Tyre.[7] As a narrative genre it sought to entertain and to instruct audiences through the oral performance of narratives that brought to life local and universal examples of exemplary conduct. Because the poems can be linked to previous Latin texts and are fairly sophisticated in their expression, drawing analogies, employing abstract terminology, and creating metaphorical and symbolic imagery to communicate their ideas, they are thought to have been composed in writing.[8] Yet the thirteenth century is a period in which oral composition continues to play an integral part of the production of written texts, even in the case of the works of renowned ecclesiastical figures such as Thomas Aquinas and Santo Martino de León, who also employed an abundance of abstract concepts and figurative language, yet dictated their texts to transcribers.

One of the more learned *cuaderna vía* poems of thirteenth-century Spain is the *Libro de Alexandre*, put into writing a generation or so after the *Cid* (Cañas 1988, 24–31). Its protagonist, Alexander of Macedonia, was featured in more than a century of verse recreations in France before appearing on parchment in Spain (Maddox and Sturm-Maddox 2002, 3–4). Its mature style, along with the lively narrative tradition that preceded it, suggest that the manuscript copy of the *Alexandre* fixes in writing one moment in the life of a narrative engaged in a continual process of oral dissemination and evolution. Clearly then, sharp distinctions between oral and written are inappropriate for the period. As René Pellen explains for the Spanish context, in the medieval period the words *auctor* 'cause, origin,' *escribir* 'to write down [what is dictated]' (Pellen 1998, 185), *texto* 'the dictated words,' as opposed to the *glosa* 'commentary or interpretation' (192), have meanings that reflect much more of a continuum between orality and writing than we would assume today. The writer of a text is a scribe who takes down the words of another, the one (or ones) who makes [*faze(n)*] the text orally. This is true for the works attributed to Alfonso X, for example, as the narrator explains in *General Estoria:*

> ... el rey faze un libro, non por quel escriua con sus manos, mas porque compone las razones del, e las emienda et yegua e enderesça, e muestra la manera de como se deuen fazer, e desi escriue las qui el manda, pero dezimos por esta razon que el rey faze el libro. (cited in Solalinde 1915, 286)[9]

> [... the King makes a book, not because he writes it with his hands, but because he composes its arguments, and he amends and measures and perfects them, and he shows the way they should be made, and in this way what he orders is written, but we say for this reason that the king makes the book.]

A good deal of scholarship on the rhymed narratives of the *mester de clerecía* has been devoted to establishing links between them and the Latin texts used in the nascent medieval university in Spain (Dutton 1973; Rico 1985; Uría 1997, xi–xiii). Yet they are vernacular texts, composed in the language shared by author and audience, no doubt intended for oral dissemination to an audience of non-clerics.[10] More to the point, vernacular narratives feature repetitions, epithets, formulas, and other expressive characteristics linked to oral composition and performance, although critics tend to view these expressive features as stylistic choices made by a writer preparing the text for oral recitation (López Guil 2001, 77–8). In part this is because in the *clerecía* narratives the link with oral production is not immediately apparent. The stricter requirements of the verse form, typically consisting of two half-lines, the first of seven syllables and the second of six, serve as a kind of metrical mould for the production of the poems, most likely constraining the poet's spontaneous production of verses. As a consequence, memory surely plays a greater role in this poetic genre than in the epic, with its looser metrical requirements.

It is not surprising that narratives produced in the context of medieval monasteries would involve memory. Monks, and learned men in general, stored vast libraries in their memories, which they retrieved in the process of making all manner of compositions (Carruthers and Ziolkowski 2002, 2–3). The memory of previous texts would be called upon in the production of the *clerecía* poems as well, and these would have been produced orally, as were the learned texts of the time. Wax tablets were employed in taking down the initial verbalization of any text, and subsequent editing would take place before making fair copy on parchment. While it is unlikely that medieval scribes would allow any examples of verbal miscues on the part of the speaker composing a prose text to reach the parchment copy, the strict metrical requirements of the *clerecía* poems would have discouraged rewriting by scribes. For this reason we may assume that the less censurable features of spontaneous oral expression would be left uncorrected in the manuscript copies of the clerical narrative poems. With this in mind, let us now scrutinize the *Fernán González* for evidence of oral composition, a centuries-old craft the *clerecía* poets and their scribes were especially proud to demonstrate.

There are circumstantial indicators in the *Fernán González* of the oral nature of composition in the period. For instance, while describing the Muslim invasion of the Iberian Peninsula in the early eighth century, the poet remarks on the incredible fact that the invaders reached Saint Martin of Tours:

Semeja fiera cosa mas dízelo el ditado,
a San Martín de Torres ovieron allegado (vv. 101c–d)[11]

[It seems an incredible thing yet the text states it,
all the way to Saint Martin of Tours they reached]

Here the poet makes reference to a dictated text – *ditado* 'dictation' – as the source of his information on the early history of Castile for the narrative. For the thirteenth century, a dictated text is a spoken text taken down by scribes, probably onto wax tablets, and eventually put to parchment. There is a subsequent reference to a dictated letter 'una carta ditada,' with a false message 'con un falso ditado' (573d). Finally, at a point in which the narrator is transitioning from one focus of narration to another, he says the following:

> Dexemos castellanos en su fuerte pesar,
> aver nos hemos luego en ellos a tornar,
> ayuntáronse en uno por se aconsejar,
> dexémoslos ayuntados, bien nos deve menbrar. (stanza 599)

> [Let us leave the Castilians in their heavy grief,
> we will have to return to them soon,
> they gathered together to counsel among themselves,
> let us leave them gathered together, we should remember it easily.]

The narrator needs to bookmark this moment clearly in order to return to it later in the narration. The bookmarking is not written, but oral. He has left the Castilians gathered together in a group, full of fear, wondering what they will do next. This strategy of leaving them in a moment of tense anticipation seems to work, for when he returns to them, they still have not agreed on a plan of action:

> dezir vos he de los castellanos, gente fuerte e ligera,
> avenir non se podian por ninguna manera (vv. 648 c–d)

> [I will tell you of the Castilians, a strong and swift people,
> in no way were they able to agree.]

There may be additional incidental indicators of orality in the text, all of which point to oral habits of thought behind the composition of the poem. But it is also apparent that any number of these indicators is not enough to convince most scholars that the poem was composed orally, because they will inevitably include them among the elements of a heritage of oral text-making that the author employs as a stylistic preference even as he composes his text in writing (Deyermond 1987, 43). To make a convincing argument for oral composition, we must be able to demonstrate that the expressive characteristics of the poem are also those of speech, as opposed to writing, and for that we can reference the features of spontaneous speech identified by Wallace Chafe, in particular the perturbations that characterize the narrative flow of a speaker as he or she experiences trouble moving from one centre of interest to another. We may recall that Chafe divides these perturbations into five categories:

1) abandonment; 2) postponement; 3) pursuit of a side interest, with subsequent return to the main track; 4) insertion of a centre of interest on a different level of interest; and 5) supplementation of a centre of interest after preliminary closure has been reached (Chafe 1980, 33). These perturbations are never immediately apparent, even for modern readers of a text, because we tend to overlook them in pursuit of meaning. For the listening audience in medieval times, it would be virtually impossible to note anything but a steady flow of meaning in the poem.

For purposes of continuity with the early portion of this chapter, we will analyse the passage that recreates the end of the battle between Almanzor and Fernán González (stanzas 264–77), which in the poem is identified as the battle of Hacinas. This is the battle of Simancas in the other texts examined in this chapter, which pitted Fernán González against his historical rival Abd al-Rahman III. In the passage the narrator is managing multiple points of view, or centres of interest, and because of this it turns out to be a fruitful place to look for perturbations in the narrative flow.

264) Por non vos detener en otras ledanías
fue Almozore vencido e todas sus cavallerías
allí fue demostrado el poder del Mexías
el conde fue David, Almozore Golías.[12]

[So as not to detain you with other litanies
Almanzor was defeated and all his warriors
there was demonstrated the power of the Messiah
the Count was David, Almanzor Goliath.]

In this first stanza, the narration of the battle is consciously abandoned, as the narrator expresses his concern that the audience not be burdened with too many details, and then simply states that Almanzor was defeated. He then steps out of the narration of the battle in order to summarize on a different level of interest, providing an abstract interpretation of the victory. Christ has prevailed, and in a metaphorical comparison, the Count is David; Almanzor is Goliath. Thus concludes the battle, or so it seems.

265) Foía almozore a guis de algarivo
diziendo '¡Ay Mafomat, en mal ora en ti fío!
non vale tres arvejas todo tu poderío.

266) El mi gran poder es muerto e cativo
pues ellos muertos son, ¿para qué finco yo viuo?'

[Almanzor fled like an outcast
saying 'Oh Mahoma, in a bad hour I believe in you!
all your power is not worth three peas

My great army is dead and captive
since they are dead, why am I still alive?']

These two stanzas are combined in some editions, in spite of the resulting imperfect end-rhyme (ivo / ío / ivo). There is some confusion
evidenced in the fact that neither stanza has the requisite four lines of
Alexandrine verse, and together they have five. Yet each stanza does
focus on a separate centre of interest. The first describes Almanzor's
anger at the prophet Mahoma, while in the second Almanzor laments
the destruction of his great army and questions his own survival. Yet,
Almanzor's speech is part of both stanzas, giving the impresssion that
they are one.

267) Fincaron en el canpo muertos muchos gentíos
de los que sanos eran aína fueron vazíos.

[On the field remained many dead people
of those who were healthy quickly they became empty.]

The narrator again changes focus, this time returning to the battlefield
to give a generic description of the many dead and the rapid retreat of
the living. The stanza seems out of place in relation to the previous description in which the narrator makes sharp distinctions between the
Muslim and Christian armies. This lack of specificity and the fact that
the stanza consists of only two verses when there should be four, suggests that the narrator is having trouble maintaining the narrative flow
as he moves from one perspective to another.

268) Quando fueron vencidos los pueblos paganos
fueron los vencedores los pueblos castellanos
el conde Fernán Gonçales con todos los cristianos
fueron en su alcance por cuestas e por los llanos.

[When the pagan people were defeated
the Castilian people were the victors
Count Fernán González with all the Christians
went in their pursuit over hills and dales.]

Here the narrator restates the result of the battle as he refocuses his attention on the pursuit of the Muslims by the Christians. This is a repetition of something already stated, not the unconscious repetition we saw in the *Cid*, since here it includes clausal subordination ('Quando fueron vencidos ...'), indicating that the narrator is aware of returning to a previous statement. Once the new focus has been established, the Christians' pursuit of the enemy ensues ('fueron en su alcance ...'), returning to the focus of 265a: 'Foía almozore a gujs de algarivo.'

269) Rendieron a Dios gracias e a Santa María
por que les dexó ver atamaña maravilla
duró les el alcance quanto medio día
enrequició del alcance por sienpre la pobre alcaldía.

[They gave thanks to God and to Holy Mary
for letting them witness such a great miracle
the chase lasted for a good half day
the poor town enriched itself forever from the chase.]

Here the Christians give thanks for their victory, which seems premature, coming as it does before the pursuit is concluded (269c). The narrator then mentions the conclusion of the pursuit and closes with the result of the Christian victory, the lasting enrichment of the victorious community. The narrator seems to be struggling between concluding the narration of the battle and moving forward, while simultaneously juggling the divergent centres of interest.

270) Quando fue Almozore gran tierra alexado
fincó de sus averes el canpo bien poblado
cojieron sus averes que Dios les avía dado
tan grande aver fallaron que non podría ser contado.

[When Almanzor was driven far away
the field was covered in his riches

they picked up his riches that God had given them
such great wealth was found that no one could count it.]

The closure of the previous stanza, in which the enrichment of the town
is mentioned (269d: 'enrequició del alcance por sienpre la pobre alcaldía'), seems to bring to mind the riches left behind on the battlefield
by the fleeing Moors. In any case, in 270a the narrator takes the audience back to the moment in which Almanzor fled (265a: 'Foía almozore
a gujs de algarivo') before mentioning the wealth left behind by the
Moors and recovered by the Christians. Closure is again suggested by
the general assessment of the amount of riches gained, which was beyond reckoning.

> 271) Fallaron en las tiendas soberano tesoro
> muchas copas e vasos que eran de vn fino oro
> nunca vio atamaña riqueza cristiano nin moro
> serien ende abondados Alexander e Poro.

> [They found great treasure in the tents
> many cups and vases that were of finest gold
> no Christian or Moor had ever seen such wealth
> Alexander and Porus would be pleased with it.]

Here the narration focuses now on a more specific assessment of the
gains already mentioned and seemingly concluded (270d: 'tan grande
aver fallaron que non podría ser contado'). Instead of continuing to
enumerate the riches, as occurs in the next strophe, the poet interrupts
this level of interest and decides to make a comparison on an abstract or
metaphorical level of interest in 271c–d ('nunca vio atamaña riqueza …
Alexandre e Poro'), once again suggesting closure.

> 272) Fallaron aí muchas maletas e muchos çurones
> llenos de oro e de plata que non de pepiones
> muchas tiendas de seda e muchos tendejones
> spadas e lorigas e muchas guarniciones.

> [They found there many chests and leather bags
> full of gold and silver and not of [coin of little value]
> many silk tents and many canopies
> swords and cuirasses and much armour.]

Here we see how after the metaphorical comparison with Alexander and Porus suggested closure, there is a return to the previous level of interest and a resumption of the description of specific material gains.

273) Fallaron aí de marfil arquetas muy preciadas
con tantas de noblezas que non podrían ser contadas
fueron para San Pedro las de aquellas dadas
están oy día en el su altar asentadas.

[They found there very precious ivory chests
with so many jewels they could never be counted
these were given to San Pedro
today they are sitting at the altar.]

The narration of specific gains continues, including a statement in 273b ('con tantas de noblezas que non podrían ser contadas') very similar to one enunciated previously in 270d ('tan grande aver fallaron que non podría ser contado'). The identification of the final destination of the battlefield booty, with a supplemental statement of contemporary witness by the narrator, leads him to comment to the audience from outside the narrative ('están oy día en el su altar asentadas' [273d]).

274) Tomaron desto todo lo que sabor ovyeron
mas quedaron aí de las dos partes que levar non lo podieron
pero las armas que fallaron dexar non las quisieron
con toda su ganancia a San Pedro venieron.

[They took away from all this what they wanted
but some from both sides remained there for they could not carry it
but the arms that they found they did not want to leave behind
with all their booty they came to San Pedro.]

Here we have a return to the narration of past events and to the battlefield, indicating that much was left behind, but not the weapons. There is also a repetition of the final destination of the booty in 274d, first stated in 273c.

275) Quando fueron aí llegados a Dios gracias rendieron
todos chicos e grandes su oración fizieron
todos por vna voca 'Deo Gratias' dixeron

cada vno sus joyas al altar las ofrecieron.

[When they arrived there they gave thanks to God
both big and small said their prayer
all in one voice said 'Deo gratias'
everyone made an offering of their jewels on the altar.]

Here the narration states the arrival at the final destination, followed by a description of thanksgiving, then a description of the placement of riches at the altar, once again emphasizing the final destination of the booty, stated earlier in 273d and 274d.

276) De toda su ganancia que Dios les avía dado
mandó tomar el quinto el conde vien aventurado
qualquier cosa que dello le copo ovo lo bien conprado
mandólo dar al monje que le diera el ospedado.

[Of all the booty that God had given them
the blessed Count ordered the taking of the fifth
whatever amount he received he had certainly earned it
he ordered it given to the monk who had taken him in as a guest.]

The narration continues with the traditional taking of a fifth of the booty by the leader, which is then turned over to the hospitable monk. The narrator once again steps out of the narration to comment on the appropriateness of the Count receiving his fifth, which constitutes an opinion at a different level of interest (276c).

277) El conde e sus gentes e todos los cruzados
a la cibdat de Burgos fueron todos aí llegados
folgaron e dormieron que eran muy cansados
demandaron maestros para sanar los llagados.

[The Count and his people and all the crusaders
to the city of Burgos all arrived there
they rested and they slept for they were very tired
they called for doctors to heal their wounds.]

Here the narration of action resumes as the Christians are depicted as crusaders and return to Burgos to rest and recuperate.

As we have seen, in the passage cited above the narrative flow is repeatedly interrupted as the narrator delivers varying perspectives on the battle, the victors and the vanquished, their Gods, and the booty recovered and eventually taken to the monastery of San Pedro de Arlanza. There are instances in which the narrator shifts focus in mid-stanza with no change in end-rhyme (264b–c, 268b–c, 269b–c, 271b–c, 273b–c), and one instance in which he shifts focus and end-rhyme (266b–267a), prompting editors to divide the four lines into two stanzas of two verses each (López-Guil 2001, 168).

These changing focuses are evidenced throughout the passage, as in stanza 264, in which the first verse indicates the abandonment of the narration of the battle, while the second verse seems to conclude the description of the battle by informing the audience that Almanzor was defeated. The narrator then introduces focuses of consciousness from another realm of interest. The first is an abstract assessment of the meaning of the Muslim defeat (264c: 'allí fue demostrado el poder del Mexías'), followed by a metaphorical comparison between the two enemies (264d: 'el conde fue David, Almozore Golías'). In neither case is the battle being described. The focus then returns to the battle, or at least to its aftermath, with the flight of Almanzor (265a), who rejects the Prophet (265b–c), and then laments the loss of his army and his own survival (266). This centre of interest is followed by two verses, each one a separate focus of consciousness, describing the battlefield covered in dead bodies (267a–b), before another centre of interest is introduced, restating the defeat of the pagans (268a: 'Quando fueron vencidos los pueblos paganos'), and reiterating, albeit in a more precise way than in 264c–d, the Christian victory (268b: 'fueron los vencedores los pueblos castellanos').

Now that the victory has been stated again, and the narrator and audience are again focused on the battle, the narrator tells of the pursuit of Almanzor by the Christians (268c–d). Next, instead of detailing the pursuit, the narrator changes focus again and relates how the Christians thanked God and Holy Mary for their victory (269a–b). Then comes a summary of the pursuit, indicating how long it lasted (269c), and, on an entirely different level of interest, seemingly in conclusion, the pursuit is said to have enriched the county of Castile for all time (269d). The narrator then returns to the pursuit (270a), much as he did with the Christian victory in 268a–b, indicating a successful conclusion before beginning the enumeration of the riches left behind.

In the description of the treasures left behind by the army of Almanzor, as in the rest of the passage, the narrator alternates between describing the booty in a material or concrete way, and commenting on it in a more abstract way, such as its provenance from God (270c) and its untold and incomparable abundance (270d, 271c–d, 273b). The references to the abundance of riches left behind suggest closure, although this occurs only in the final instance, itself a fairly close repetition of the first instance (270d: 'tan grande aver fallaron que non podría ser contado'; 273b: 'con tantas de noblezas que non podrían ser contadas'). The narrator also relates the transfer of the riches to the monastery of San Pedro de Arlanza twice (273c–d, 274d), before reiterating the arrival of the Christians to San Pedro (275a), in a fashion similar to the reiteration of the Christian victory (268a–b), and of the pursuit of Almanzor (270a). More than simple repetitions, these reiterations seem to be a way for the narrator to keep actions in his and the audience's mind while focusing attention on the subsequent centre of interest.

The description of this passage, following Wallace Chafe in his linking of speech characteristics to human consciousness, helps us follow the narrator's changing focus as he relates different perspectives on several actions occurring nearly simultaneously. Although not all five categories of perturbations that Chafe identifies in his study are evidenced here, surely a case can be made for (c) Pursuit of a side interest (269a–b), with subsequent return to the main track (269c–d); (d) Insertion of a centre of interest on a different level of interest (264c–d, 271c–d, 273c–d); and (e) Supplementation of a centre of interest after preliminary closure has been reached (267a–b). As in the examples Chafe provides, some repetition results from the movement from one centre of interest to another.

Repetitions occur when the narrator makes a definitive break from one setting to another, a transition that requires significant reorientation. The narrator seems to have an established protocol for communicating this reorientation, as all three instances are strikingly similar: when the focus moves from the battle to the chase (268a–b), from the chase to the retrieval of the booty left on the battlefield (270a–b), and when the Castilians transition from the battlefield to the monastery of San Pedro (275a). When we are told that the pagans lost the battle and the Castilians won (268a–b), we already know it, as we already know that Almanzor was driven far away (270a–b), and that the Castilians went to San Pedro (275a). Chafe finds the greatest amount of hesitation in his speakers when they are compelled to reorient themselves in time or space while moving from one centre of interest to another. As he puts it, 'It is harder to find a new perch when the background for the perch must first be established' (Chafe 1980, 44).

The hesitation that Chafe was able to measure in the speech of his subjects is of course not evidenced in the parchment copy of this thirteenth-century poem, but there does seem to be an established protocol for easing into transitions from one centre of interest to another. In the three cases of repetition cited above, the narrator employs a simple reiterative formula based on the use of *quando* (when), as in 'Quando fueron vençidos los pueblos paganos' (268a), 'Quando fue Almozore gran tierra alexado' (270a), and 'Quando fueron aí llegados' (275a). This technique, by reiterating a past action as concluded, serves to re-situate the narration on a new centre of interest or, as Chafe would have it, to establish the background for a new perch. From this new perch the narration can proceed, which is precisely what takes place in all three instances.

The repeated use of this technique suggests that the narrator has developed a way through the cognitive constraints of spontaneous narration, for himself and his audience. As he transitions from one scene to the next, and from one level of discourse to another, he seems to be well aware that he is restating actions, much like the oral bookmark he placed earlier in the narration, in stanza 599, cited above. The techniques employed in the *Cid* are not as sophisticated. In the best-known case of simultaneous actions in the *Cid* – the three judicial duels of Fernando, Diego, and Asur González against the Cid's men –the poet, after describing individually two of the duels, simply states, 'Los dos han arrancado, dirévos de Muño Gustioz' [The first two have charged, I'll tell you of Muño Gustioz] (l. 3671). In this case, the poet pretends to be narrating three actions simultaneously, but in fact he narrates them successively. The poet of the *Mocedades de Rodrigo*, an epic poem to be examined in the next chapter, simply narrates successively, with not even the pretence of managing simultaneous actions.

Another way to appreciate the way in which the cognitive constraints of oral verse-making contribute to the unique expression of epic poetry is to examine a poetic passage that has been transferred to prose. This is possible in the case of most of the *Fernán González* because the compilers of Alfonso X's *Estoria de España* included a good deal of the poem in their prose history (Bailey 1996, 31). As noted earlier, the Alfonsine chroniclers translated orally their Arabic source texts as scribes took down the translations in dictation. In the case of the *Fernán González* and other vernacular verse texts, we may assume that oral dictation was employed in the early stages of its transfer to prose, yet the final copy suggests that significant editorial intervention followed dictation, since the prose text is free of the changing perspectives of the poem.

> ... que vençieron todo el poder de los moros, e fuyó Almançor con muy pocos caualleros. E ally mostró Dios aquel día su poder qual era de vençer trezientos caualleros a tan gran gentío de moros e tan poderoso como Almançor. [Ca Almançor era en lugar de enperador entre los moros e teníanlo como su señor, e llamauánle por su arábigo Ally Agili, que quiere tanto dezir como 'pestaña guarda el ojo'; asy guardaua él e defendía su gente.] Pues que los moros fueron vençidos e fuyeron del canpo, e fue el conde Fernán Gonçáles en pos ellos en alcançe con algunos de los suyos, e mató muchos dellos, e los otros que fincaron rrobaron el canpo e fallaron en las tiendas muchas arcas llenas de oro e de plata, muchos basas e armas e otras noblezas muchas; asy que enrrequiçieron todos además para siempre. Des y fuese el conde con todos los suyos para el monesterio de Sant Pedro, e dio y muchas de aquellas noblezas que fallaran en las tiendas de los moros, e dio tan grande algo al monje cuyo huesped él fuera. Después que esto ouo fecho, fuese para Burgos e folgó y él e su conpaña y quantos días, e mandó catar maestros para guaresçer los que eran feridos. (*Crónica de veinte reyes* 90, col. 1 [Libro II, cap. 7])[13]

> [... they defeated the army of the Moors, and Almanzor excaped with very few warriors. And there God showed that day the reach of his power as three hundred knights defeated such a great multitude of Moors and the powerful Almanzor. [For Almanzor had the place of emperor among the Moors whose lord he was, and they called him in Arabic Ally Agili, which means 'eyelash protects the eye'; as he protected and defended his people.] Since the Moors were defeated and fled from the field, Count Fernán González went in pursuit of them with some of his men, and killed many of them, and those whose remained behind pillaged the field and found in the tents many chests full of gold and silver, many vases and arms and many other riches; such that they all became rich forever more. Then the Count with all his men went to the monastery of San Pedro, and gave there many of the riches they found in the tents of the Moors, and he gave great wealth to the monk whose guest he had been. After he did this, he went to Burgos and he and his men rested there some days, and he had doctors brought in to heal those who were wounded.]

Immediately apparent is the absence of the paratactic structure characteristic of speech and of oral narrative poetry. Compared to the poem, this narration seems nearly seamless as it transtions through the sequence of events, employing hypotactic syntax to coordinate the various actions described. There is none of the fitful jumping back and forth between centres of interest found in the poem as the text relates actions that occur more or less simultaneously. There is a change in focus as the narration moves from events to commenting on them ('And there God showed ...' [line 2]), yet it is barely noticeable here in its single occurrence.

Also apparent is a very distinctive ideological thrust. Unlike the poem, here Almanzor's stature is preserved even in defeat, while the role of God in the victory is mentioned only once, thus heightening the role of the Castilian warriors in the victory. This perspective brings into clearer focus the existence of a meta-narrative conception of the poem. The narrator has come to understand the story in a way unique to his own circumstances, most probably as part of a religious community at the monastery of San Pedro de Arlanza, with its documented connections to the historical Fernán González and the resting place of his mortal remains (Salvador Martínez 1991, 10, 22–3).

It is precisely the impulse to explain the meaning of the poem while narrating heroic deeds that produces the narrative perturbations discussed above. Yet, by delivering an interpretation of those deeds to his audience, the narrator establishes a kind of dialogue between the subject of the narration, a battlefield victory of the tenth century, and an audience of the thirteenth century. The references that attempt to bridge that time span, and in essence facilitate the dialogue between the past and a contemporary audience, are the key to understanding the narrator's expectation of his audience and of the meaning they wished to find in the poem.

1) 264d: el conde fue David, Almozore Golías.

This first example can be understood as a simple metaphorical comparison, but it also must have activated in the audience a deeper connection to the story of Fernán González by referencing the more familiar, and surely more meaningful, biblical story of David and Goliath.

2) 271d: serien ende abondados Alexander e Poro.

Another metaphorical comparison, this time to the story of Alexander the Great, popular in Spain and throughout Europe at the time. Through these two comparisons the poet is indicating to his audience the transcendence of the achievements of Fernán González.

The next example links the glorious past of Fernán González to the present-day monastery of San Pedro de Arlanza, familiar to audience and poet, where the remains of the hero lay and where the text was most likely put to parchment (López Guil 2001, 25; Salvador Martínez 1991, 23):

3) 273c–d: fueron para San Pedro las de aquellas dadas
estan oy día en el su altar asentadas.

In the final example Fernán González and his Castilian warriors are called crusaders ('cruzados'):

4) 277a–b: El conde e sus gentes e todos los cruzados
a la cibdat de Burgos fueron todos aí llegados.

Since the Fernán González of history is known to us through documents dating from 929 to 945 (Salvador Martínez 1991, 9–16), more than one hundred years before the First Crusade was launched by Pope Urban II in 1095, we may assume that the narrator is either confused or is attempting to link the battlefield victory of his hero to his own present circumtances and those of his audience. In fact, as López Guil points out, the portrayal in the poem of Fernán González and his Castilian warriors as crusaders suggests that the monastic culture was keenly in tune with the tenor of the times, specifically with the fact that Pope Innocent IV wrote to the bishops of Cartagena and Zamora, Spain (4 October 1252), providing them with guidelines for gathering funds for an expedition to free Christian captives in Morroco. On 10 January 1253, this same pope ordered Franciscans and Dominicans to preach the Crusade in Navarre, León, and Castile, and on 4 August 1254, he received under the special protection of the Holy See the crusaders of Castile and León (López-Guil 2001, 32, especially note 31).

These facts suggest that the narrator of the poem wished to update the story of Fernán González, making the hero and his deeds relevant to the crusader currents of his time. Two allusions to references outside the story, the biblical story of David and Goliath, and the wealth won in the defeat of Porus by Alexander the Great, support the portrayal of Fernán González as fighting for God, and of the riches to be gained in fighting the Muslims, respectively. Another allusion recalls the ivory chests that Fernán González won in his battlefield victory over the Muslim general Almanzor and donated to the monastery of San Pedro, where they still sit before the altar (strophe 273). Other statements contribute to the crusader sense, such as attributing the victory to God (264c, 269a–b, 270c, 275a–d, 276a), and Almanzor's recognition that the Prophet has no power over the Christians (265b–c). The reference to the donation to the monastery of the two ivory chests filled with treasure (273c), and of other battlefield riches (275d), as well as the payment of one-fifth of the booty to the monk who had sheltered Fernán González (276d), portray the monastery as the source of the divine force guiding Fernán González in his battlefield victory.

Together these allusions contribute to an updating of the story of Fernán González, an effort by the narrator to tell the traditional story, but through extra-narrative allusions. He seems intent on crafting a new image of the hero that conforms to the lived reality and concerns of his audience, and reflects a monastic inspiration and perhaps even the setting for the performnce of the poem. Clearly then, the story is being revised, but here the revisions are seemingly spontanenous comments or reflections interspersed in the narration. Yet the coherence of the allusions suggests that they comprise a unified vision of the hero and of the role of the monastery in his success. To some degree they must have been premeditated and vetted by the monastic community of San Pedro, which would have participated in the formulation of this narrative renewal of the meaning of the deeds of the Castilian warrior so closely linked to their monastery.

The references to David and Goliath and to Alexander and Porus seem highly literary, yet they may be explained in relation to the monastic practice of *collatio*, an oral process in which a monastic community engages in an exercise of communal bringing together of texts, through reading and conversations about them, a 'feeding upon texts as one feeds at a community meal' (Carruthers 1990, 217). This process imbued the traditional epic tale of *Fernán González* with new meaning, associating his battlefield successes with the early monastery of San Pedro de Arlanza and the hermit monk Pelayo who sheltered the hero in his time of need. Like Alexander, who gained untold wealth through his conquests, and like the young David, who defeated and killed the Philistine giant, Fernán González won great riches and enduring fame through his battle with Almanzor. The monastery of San Pedro channelled God's support to the Castilians, and they, in turn, rewarded the monastery and its hermit monk Pelayo with untold wealth.

These revisions in the Fernán González story bring to mind Bakhtin's undertsanding of the epic as 'walled off absolutely from all subsequent times, and above all from those times in which the singer and his listeners are located' (Bakhtin 1981, 15–16). Its discourse is 'impossible to change, to re-think, to re-evaluate anything in it. It is completed, conclusive and immutable, as a fact, an idea and a value' (17). In the recasting of the *Fernán González*, the San Pedro monks accomplished a significant feat of their own: they imagined a place for themselves in the crusader currents of their time, based on their role in earlier wars against the Muslims. A traditional epic tale on Fernán González was familiar to them, but as they assimilated the story through readings and reflections, it ceased being an artefact and took on a new and more relevant meaning as it was '"collated" with its multitude of readers' (Carruthers 1990, 217). Even though Bakhtin defines the epic as walled off, it is precisely a dialogue with an epic past that allows the monks of San Pedro to re-imagine themselves as participants in the crusader currents of their time. They are able to recreate an epic past for their monastery, link it to the present, and in so doing position themselves directly in the midst of the most significant event of their time. As Brian Stock might have it, in the creation of a new discourse about the past, the monks of San Pedro are 'transcending, and yet incorporating, the past' (Stock 1990, 171).

A final insight into the compositional process employed in refashioning the epic tale of Fernán González can be found in an episode in which Fernán González and his army of Castilian warriors are about to face the scourge of Christian Spain, the Muslim general Almanzor. The Count makes his way to San Pedro in the dark of night only to find that the saintly hermit who had counselled him earlier has died. Full of fear and dread at the thought of his impending defeat and death at the hands of the infidel, the Count falls to his knees in tearful prayer as he begs God for assistance.

In his prayer he describes the sorry state of the Christian leadership and the treaties they have signed with the Muslim leaders in their desire to avoid war. He mentions one biblical text, the book of Isaiah, a prophet who also lived through political turmoil and refused to compromise his faith in God, exhorting his people to remain true to the 'God of hosts' (Isaiah 10:24). Fernán González shows that he has assimilated this text and embodies its teachings as he prays and describes to God his role as the one true Christian vassal, alone in his fight against the Muslims.

Por las escrituras que dixo Yssayas,
que a los tus vasallos nunca los falescerías,

Señor tu sieruo so con miz cavallerías,
non me partiré de ti en todos los mis días (stanza 396)

[Because of the scriptures that Isaiah spoke,
that you would never fail your vassals,
Lord I am your servant with my knights,
I will not abandon you in all my days.]

Note that Fernán González knows the text as written, but assumes that
the prophet Isaiah spoke the words preserved in the text. He invokes
God's aid, and his intense prayer eventually leads to sleep:

Teniendo su vegilía con Dios se razonando,
vn sueño muy sabroso el conde fue tomando,
con sus armas guarnido asy se fue acostando,
la carne adormida así yaze soñando (399)

[Having his vigil speaking with God,
a very deep sleep began to overtake the Count,
with his arms on he began to lie down,
with his flesh asleep he lies dreaming.]

During his sleep, Fernán González is first visited by the recently de-
ceased Pelayo, referred to now as a saint (San Pelayo), who offers assurances that God recognizes him as his loyal vassal and that he will
defeat the enemy of his faith and should go now to make war against
Almanzor. As he is waking from this dream, Fernán González hears
another voice telling him not to delay, then mapping out a battle plan,
telling the count to divide his forces into three groups, attacking from
the east, the west, and the north. This voice tells him that he will be
joining Fernán González in the battle, as will Saint James (Santiago),
the patron saint of Spain:

Entre la otra tercera de partes de aquilóm,
venceremos si esto tú fazes a este vravo leóm,
ffarás tú si esto fazes a guissa de Sansón,
quando con las manos lidió con el vestióm (411)

[Have the other third enter from the north,
we will win if you do this to this fierce lion,

you will be, if you do this, like Samson,
when with his hands he fought with the beast.]

The speaker then reveals himself to be Saint Emilianus (San Millán),
the much revered saint from the nearby monastery named for him, sent
to Fernán González by Jesus Christ. This knowledge affords Fernán
González new confidence with which he can now return to his en-
camped forces and convince them to take up the battle against the
seemingly overwhelming enemy forces:

Non quiero más dezir te, por ende lieva dende, ve tu vía,
¿quieres saber quién trae esta mensajería?
Millán so por nonbre, Jhesu Xristo me enbía. (412)

[I don't want to tell you more, so get up, be on your way,
Do you want to know who brings this message?
Millán is my name, Jesus Christ sends me.]

Quando ovo don Fernando todo esto oído,
el varón don Millán a los cielos fue ido,
fue luego el buen conde de la ermita espedido,
tornó se a Piedra Fitta donde él fuera salido. (413)

[When don Fernando heard this,
the noble don Millán went up to the heavens,
the good Count soon left the hermitage [San Pedro],
he returned to Piedra Fita whence he came.]

The new confidence that Fernán González takes with him provides
the conviction he needs to rally his men to battle the next day:

Quando ovo el conde dichas estas razones,
antes tenien todos endurecidos los coraçones,
fueron todos confortados cavalleros e peones,
mandó commo fiziesen esos grandes varones (443)

[When the Count had finished his explanations,
before they all had hardened hearts,
knights and footsoldiers were all comforted,
he ordered these great nobles into action.]

The vision that comforted Fernán González and his men in their time of turmoil began with fear or dread, then intense meditation or prayer, followed by communion with the divine (the vision or visitation), and finally a return to the everyday world with new knowledge or confidence. This new knowledge is then shared with his men, as he relates to them the promise of victory over Almanzor (stanzas 421–4). The comparison of Fernán González to Samson, the biblical hero, like the reference to the words of the prophet Isaiah, is evidence of a monastic compositional process in which 'past authors are constantly related in and through present minds' (Carruthers 1990, 193–4). Fernán González is not composing, of course, although his vision recreates the medieval practice of monastic visionary invention employed for centuries in European monasteries, where the act of composing began with a state of unease or anxiety. Concentrated memory work would follow, such as the reciting of psalms or other memorized texts. The revoicing of these texts, either silently or aloud, leads to vision, which is the activity of composing, and results in the writing down of a new literary work (Carruthers 1998, 183).

The depiction of this specialized rhetorical practice in the *Fernán González* suggests an expansion of monastic habits of idea-making and composition, from closed monastic communities in the eleventh century to an engagement with royal courts and noble households well into the thirteenth century. While the original story was based on historical events, the references to biblical stories and other written texts were added later as the poem was re-imagined by a monk or a group of monks through a process much like the one that induced the prophetic vision of the hero of the poem. This process involved a sense of fear or dread, or maybe nothing more than weeping at the prospect of composition, followed by prayer, which could easily take the form of reciting the psalms silently or communally out loud. Familiar prayers or biblical passages might also be recalled, all of which would lead to a vision, as with the hero, and to a new way of envisioning him. In this case the vision included seeing the hero in prayer, referencing the words of the prophet Isaiah and imagining himself the lone defender of the true God, unwilling to compromise with the Muslim menace.

Fernán González woke from his prophetic vision with new confidence and returned to his men to tell them of the assurances he had received of divine assistance and final victory against the enemy. The monks who envisioned a new Fernán González emerging from a combination of legendary deeds and a storehouse of memorized texts probably arose satisfied from their vision of the hero transcribed onto wax tablets for later editing and placement on parchment, just as with any other composition (Carruthers 1990, 204). Once they were satisfied with the product of these cogitations, they would want to preserve them as a text for study, future meditation, and maybe even for communal reading, including the crusaders they no doubt wished to inspire. The Fernán González they created was made in their own image. He was dedicated fully to God, had no use for temporal power or worldly riches, and when he was troubled by the heavy burden placed on him by God, he would resort to prayer at the religious shrine that had since become their monastery. From all this it seems reasonable to assume that the monks took very seriously their recreation of Fernán González. The hero they imagined through familiar texts was surely meant to provide comfort, to them and to others confronting challenges in a time of great change and uncertainty.

Like the *Fernán González*, the *Mocedades de Rodrigo* (the young Cid) is an epic poem that includes the foundational narrative of a religious shrine. Like the *Cid*, the *Mocedades* presents us with a warrior hero who does not identify in any appreciable way with monastic sensibilities. The narrator is not as sophisticated in his expression or in the overall design of his narrative as the poet of the *Fernán González* and was most likely not familiar with monastic rhetorical practices. But the way the poem was put together, both in its initial composition and in its placement on parchment, is of interest to us and will be fully examined in chapter 5.

5 The *Mocedades de Rodrigo*

The *Mocedades de Rodrigo* is an epic poem that narrates the youthful deeds of the adolescent Rodrigo Díaz, better known in later life as the Cid. In this narrative the protagonist is the descendant of legendary warrior lords who governed Castile in times of continual aggression. The heroine is the daughter of a count, killed in retaliatory combat by the young hero. Their marriage is imposed, meant to appease the need for vengeance in the recent blood feud and to save the king from disrupting the uneasy alliance between the Castilian and Leonese factions of his kingdom. The story is also about the initiation of a young man into adulthood, and the role of women in that process. Jimena demands Rodrigo's hand in marriage and so makes him part of a community larger than his extended family and their alliances. Initially he is full of bravura, but this attitude masks insecurities about his social stature and the fear that he may not measure up to the king and the counts of his court. Rodrigo must face up to these insecurities and transcend the ties of his youth to earn a place as the king's most trusted warrior in the service of his country. He accomplishes this through a series of battlefield victories, culminating in his leadership of the combined forces of all the kingdoms of Spain in their invasion of France. The ending of the poem is most likely missing from the manuscript, but we may presume that Rodrigo returned to his homeland in triumph, married the woman who compelled him to think big, and went on to fulfil his destiny as the most celebrated warrior in the history of Spain (Hook and Long 1999, 66–7).

It should be clear even from this brief outline that the *Mocedades* is a compelling story with mythic resonances reaching well beyond the particulars of Rodrigo's youth. Thomas Montgomery has established substantial episodic and sequential links between the *Mocedades*, as well as the French *Tristan* and the Spanish *Siete infantes de Lara*, and a pan-European initiation myth first evidenced in the Irish epic hero Cúchulainn, as portrayed in the great saga *Táin Bó Cúailnge*, whose fragments date from the eighth to the twelfth centuries (Montgomery 1998, 11–41; 1999). Like Rodrigo, Cúchulainn proves himself an exceptionally fierce warrior, to the extreme of menacing his own people, before being assimilated back into society through the mediation of one or more women.[1] Additional resonances with the *Mocedades* are evident in another narrative that pre-dates it, the epic tale of Bernardo del Carpio, first recorded in the *Chronicon mundi* (ca 1236), and soon after, in a somewhat variant version, in the *De Rebus Hispanie* (ca 1242), reviewed earlier in chapter 2. Like Rodrigo in the *Mocedades*, in these narratives Bernardo rises to the defence of Spain against the threatening Franks, in this case a Carolingian incursion of the late eighth century. Bernardo desecrates the invading army, killing Roland, the valiant hero of the *Chanson de Roland*.[2] Although direct influence from these narratives is not verifiable in a material way, the connections are difficult to ignore, as they enhance the appeal of the poem by expanding its traditional basis.

Episodes from the *Mocedades* have echoes in other texts that pre-date the poem, but these are more conventional in that they treat Rodrigo's youth directly. The first of these is from his own lifetime, the Latin panegyric *Carmen Campidoctoris* (ca 1083), which enthusiastically celebrates Rodrigo's exploits in the field of battle.[3] This anonymous poem briefly mentions Rodrigo's noble lineage and then recounts his youthful triumph over a Navarrese warrior. This victory leads the more seasoned veterans to call him 'Campeador,' and it presages his greatness in the field of battle later in life. The poem also tells of the esteem in which the young Rodrigo was held by Castilian King Sancho II, and of his desire to reward him, and, after Sancho's untimely death, the warm welcome extended him by Alfonso VI. The subsequent episodes are not of Rodrigo's youth, and are treated in more detail in the *Cid*, but the poem leaves little doubt that during the hero's own lifetime, his youth had become the subject of legendary acclaim.

Written in prose, but no less admirable, are the episodes from Rodrigo's youth recorded in the *Historia Roderici*, a Latin prose biography of Rodrigo Díaz that also pre-dates the *Mocedades* by more than a century.[4] The narration of his youthful deeds begins with his upbringing in the household of King Sancho II of Castile and his girding with the belt of knighthood. It notes his participation in the battle of Graus, in which Sancho killed King Ramiro I of Aragon, his own uncle. Sancho later makes Rodrigo commander of his army and standard-bearer in the battles he fought against his brother Alfonso VI, king of León. In a legendary fight during Sancho's siege of Zamora, young Rodrigo is attacked by fifteen enemy combatants, seven of them wearing chain mail. He kills one of them, unhorses two, and with his spirited courage sends the remainder into flight. He later fought and defeated Jimeno Garcés, a renowned warrior from Pamplona (the Navarrese warrior of the *Carmen*), and defeated and killed a Saracen at Medinaceli. After Sancho's death, his brother Alfonso received him honourably into his court and gave him as wife one of his relatives, the lady Jimena, the daughter of the Count of Oviedo (Falque 1990, 48–9, chaps 4–6; Barton and Fletcher 2000, 100–1).

These two Latin texts present details that appear later in the *Mocedades* and others that do not. Unlike the *Mocedades*, they assign Rodrigo's early deeds to his service of Sancho II of Castile, and after his untimely death, Rodrigo serves King Alfonso VI. A detail they both share with the later *Mocedades* is his singular victory over a renowned warrior from Navarre. The vernacular *Estoria de España* (ca 1284) includes brief references to episodes of Rodrigo's youth that are best explained as reflecting at least three distinct oral narratives (Armistead 2000, 37).[5] In these episodes the young Rodrigo is portrayed as a warrior in the service of King Fernando I, father of Sancho II. This change is significant, as it runs counter to the previous Latin texts and presages the vassal-lord relationship in the *Crónica de Castilla* (ca 1290).[6] This vernacular chronicle intersperses throughout the reign of Fernando I the youthful deeds of Rodrigo that are later narrated sequentially in the *Mocedades* (Armistead 2000, 39–40).

Although there are common threads in the varied narratives of Rodrigo's youth, the protagonist of the *Mocedades* marks a sharp transition in its portrayal of Rodrigo as extremely independent and belligerent, especially in his relationship with King Fernando, essentially his co-protagonist in the poem. Fernando also undergoes an unexpected transformation in the poem. While in chronicles and the early passages of the poem he is portrayed as a decisive and powerful leader, once he is paired with the young Rodrigo, Fernando becomes a weak and ineffectual child-king. These transformations have led critics to see the historically unfortunate minorities of Fernando IV (1295–1301) and Alfonso XI (1312–25) as responsible for inducing the collective Castilian imagination into portraying a pathetic Fernando as the youthful co-dependent of a domineering Rodrigo.

One way to understand this process is to imagine poet and audience attempting to recreate the traditional story of Rodrigo's youth under the tutelage of a mature and powerful King Fernando I. As the strikingly inept minority of Fernando IV bore into the collective consciousness, the narrative gradually began to incorporate the lived reality of an incompetent king, also named Fernando. In response to these conditions, young Rodrigo's legendary precociousness grew in order to compensate for the perceived incompetence of his king. Eventually this process yielded a narrative in which Fernando is depicted first as a decisive and honoured leader of men (akin to the historical Fernando I), but in the company of the force of nature that is the twelve-year-old Rodrigo, Fernando becomes a cowering and indecisive child-king unable to protect his kingdom from domestic and foreign aggression (reminiscent of Fernando IV), and entirely dependent on Rodrigo. A reasonable estimation of this process places its starting point prior to the premature death of Fernando IV in 1312. It would have run its course by the time the equally wrenching minority of Alfonso XI came to an end in 1325 (Martin 1992, 471). The extant version of the *Mocedades* probably reflects this transformative process near its beginning, since the positive portrayal of Fernando still seems relevant.

Clearly the story of the Cid's youth was a subject of speculation from the time he began to demonstrate his battlefield prowess. Early texts testify to its importance while later versions point to a vibrant literary culture engaging its heroic past through received narratives and reinterpreting them in accordance with new social circumstances. The story that emerged was so powerful that some interests sought to enhance their own status by insinuating themselves into the life of the hero and the deeds of his youth, while others simply wanted to leave their mark on the narration of those deeds. The most significant of these insinuations involves the interpolation in the first half of the poem of four passages that narrate episodes of the legendary history of the diocese of Palencia. No attempt was made to blend this material into the pre-existing text, causing noticeable interruptions in the narrative flow of the poem. A genealogy of the Laínez family, Rodrigo's father and paternal uncles, with no perceptible rhyme scheme has also been carelessly inserted into the text of the poem. And finally, titles and patronymics were added to a number of lines, entirely disrupting their traditional rhythm. Together these interventions reveal an exceptional disregard for the coherence, flow, and rhythm of the poem. They surely required a meta-narrative perspective capable of viewing the text from a distance, as an object for manipulation, all of which is the province of the learned.

In reviewing then, what we seem to have in the extant text of the *Mocedades* is a narrative based on traditional themes but with timely adaptations that imbued it with renewed vigour and relevance. Its continued relevance is supported by evidence that learned clerics, or at least certainly not poets, attempted to insinuate themselves into the narrative by interpolating their own story into that of the young Rodrigo. Although scholars are generally able to discern the presence of these two clearly demarcated elements in the extant text of the poem, the traditional themes versus the learned interpolations, there is general consensus that the poem was composed in writing. After reviewing the prevailing notions on the manner of its composition, I will venture to offer some new analytical tools that should allow us a more nuanced view of the poem's composition.

Among all scholars, Leonardo Funes has made the most sustained examination of the structure of the extant text and finds that it represents at least three separate redactions. The first redaction would have occurred towards the end of the thirteenth century and contained the early history of Castile and story of Rodrigo's youth (Funes 2004, xxxviii). A second redaction produced an entirely new text with the addition of the legendary material on the foundation of the diocese of Palencia. Funes believes that this copy was produced early in the fourteenth century, during the reign of Fernando IV (xxxiv, lix). A final redaction inserted a genealogy of Rodrigo's family and lengthened verses through the addition of family names, titles, and so forth. A chronicler, much like the author of the Portuguese *Livro das linaghens*, made this final copy at the very end of the fourteenth century, resulting in the extant text (xxxiii, lx). Although his findings are based on the work of a number of scholars, Funes summarizes their work in an even-handed manner while adding well-reasoned observations of his own.

In Funes's formulation, then, the majority of the text, the history of early Castile and Rodrigo's *mocedades*, was put to parchment near the end of the thirteenth century, while the Palencia material was added a short time later by a cleric associated with that diocese. Deyermond does not distinguish between compositional levels in the extant text and attributes the composition of the entire poem to a Palencia cleric. Montgomery outlines the evidence for a number of hands participating in the composition of the extant text over an extended period of time. All three scholars acknowledge the traditional nature of most of the poetic material, with the possible exception of the Palencia legend. They also agree that the compositional stages involved writing, and not oral dictation by a minstrel to a scribe (Funes 2004, liii; Deyermond 1969, 201, esp. note 19; 1999, 11–12; Montgomery 1984b, 132–3).

The prevailing view of the learned nature of the extant text seems accurate. What is open to question is the assumption that accompanies that view, that learned authorship necessarily means a text composed in writing, and not a dictated oral text: 'el manuscrito existente no debe nada a un manuscrito dictado' (Deyermond 1999, 14). The thematic coherence of the *Mocedades* is certainly attributable to a learned mindset, someone capable of pulling together diverse materials to create a master narrative where nothing similar had existed before. Rather than challenge that assumption, I would like to shift the focus of attention away from its organization on parchment to its expression, to speak not about its theme and purpose as a composition, but about its relationship to speech and to its composition through dictation to a scribe.

The poor expressive quality of the poem has led scholars to conclude that what may have once been a traditional text, can best be described in its current form as the unfortunate result of heavy-handed clerical intervention. Among the indicators of its weakened expressivity is the fact that many of the verses are excessively long for traditional epic phrasing. Some eighty of these verses betray a chronicler's concern for adding titles and complete names to otherwise perfectly acceptable epic verses. In other instances nouns designating family relationships and deliberate stylistic archaisms have been added. Another indication of the poem's lack of expressive vitality is the repeated use of the *á-o* assonance in over 80 per cent of its verses (Montgomery 1984a, 12). The verses include formulas, but these are deployed in a transparently mechanical way, while adjective use seems conventional and automatic when compared with the resonance and restraint of the *Cid* (Montgomery 1993, 175). Perhaps the most troubling of all the poem's weaknesses is the way the poem presents its most compelling episodes, in that some of these lose their dramatic effect through a series of disconcerting breaks in the narrative flow.

Even more surprising to some scholars is the fact that the first folio of the poem is not verse at all. It narrates a legendary history of early Castile structured through the repetition of *e(t)* [and] at the beginning of each idea unit. Typically, editors of the poem treat this first folio as prose, dividing it into paragraphs, even though the manuscript is not structured in this way. They do this because the learned vernacular prose texts of the period, the Alfonsine chronicles, rely heavily on the repetition of *e(t)*, and so specialists assume that this structuring device signals a learned composition, by which they mean a text composed in writing (Webber 1980, 206).

Let us take another look at this assumption. First of all, we know that both Latin and vernacular prose histories drew from the oral narratives of minstrels, because their authors tell us so (Fernández Valverde 1987, 128 [Liber IIII, cap. X]; Fradejas Lebrero 1991, 36–7). We also know that oral dictation to a scribe writing on wax tablets was a common form of composition for all manner of texts in the medieval period. The difference between transcribing a learned composition and one less so, including an oral narrative, is a matter of degrees of correction. The compositions of learned men and of minstrels alike were conveyed orally through dictation to a scribe, while a learned composition would be subjected to further stages of editing in the process of transferring the text from wax tablets to fair copy (Carruthers 1990, 194–6). Understood in this way, when we look to distinguish oral composition from texts composed in writing, we should be alert to markers of corrective editing imposed on an orally dictated text.

We now know that among the most significant markers of oral discourse is the preference of speakers for an adjoining (each idea unit is treated syntactically as an independent unit) or coordinating strategy (idea units are linked together with coordinating conjunctions, usually 'and,' less often 'then,' 'but,' or 'so') over the use of subordination in written discourse, as Chafe outlines it for us.[7] Before returning to the *Mocedades*, let us look at the first vernacular prose history compiled in Spain, the *Liber regum* (ca 1200), written in Navarrese, which also employs *e(t)* frequently as a structuring device, especially when it narrates sequential actions, as in the following example:

> Est rei don Alfonso non lexo fillo nenguno, ni non remaso omne de so lignage qui mantouiesse el reismo, & estido la tierra assi luengos tiempos. E pues acordoron se & eslieron dos iudices porque s' cabdellassen d'estos dos iudices: el uno ouo nomne Nunno Rasuera e el otro ouo nomne Lain Calbo. Del lignage de Nunno Rasuera uino l'emperador de Castiella, e del lignage de Lain Calbo uino mio Çith el Campiador. (Cooper 1960, 33)

> [This king Alfonso left no son, nor did any man of his lineage remain who might defend the realm, and the land was like this for many years. And so they gathered and elected two judges so that they might be led by these

two judges: one was named Nuño Rasuera and the other was named Laín
Calvo. From the lineage of Nuño Rasuera came the emperor of Castile,
and from the lineage of Laín Calvo came Mio Cid the Campeador.]

This passage displays the compositional strategies of spontaneous
speech, with an abundance of coordinating conjunctions: '& estido la
tierra assi luengos tiempos. E pues acordoron se and eslieron dos iudices' [and the land was like this for many years. And so they gathered
and elected two judges]. It also exhibits the more complex syntax of
written texts: 'ni non remaso omne de so lignage qui mantouiesse el
reismo' [nor did any man of his lineage remain who might defend the
realm]; 'eslieron dos iudices porque s' cabdellassen d'estos dos iudices'
[they elected two judges so that they might be led by these two judges].
There is also a strong tendency toward parallelism, as in 'el uno ouo
nomne ... eel otro ouo nomne,' 'Del lignage de ... uino, del lignage de
... uino,' with frequent use of *et* and & (a common abbreviation for *e(t)*)
to join clauses and for transition to new ideas. The passage bears some
examples of the subordination or syntactic integration of learned prose,
while the parallelistic structure and the abundant use of *et* also suggest
oral composition, precisely the combination of expressive strategies we
would expect from a text composed orally and subsequently corrected.

The first folio of the *Mocedades* contains a passage on the same subject
as the passage cited from the *Liber regum*, but it shows less subordination and more of the parallelistic structure and the accumulation of coordinating conjunctions identified by Chafe as markers of conversational
spoken language (Chafe and Danielwicz 1987, 16–18):

E porque los castellanos ivan a cortes al rey de León con fijas e mugieres,
    por esta razón fizieron en Castilla dos alcaldes,
e quando fuesse el uno a la corte, que'l otro manparasse la tierra.
¿Quáles fueron estos alcaldes?
El uno fue Nuño Rasura e el otro Laín Calvo.
¿E por qué dixieron Nuño Rasura este nonbre? Porque cogió de Castilla
    señas eminas de pan,
e fizo voto a Santiago que les ayudasse contra los moros. (Bailey 2007, lines
    12–19)

[And because the Castilians went to the king of León's court with their
    daughters and wives,
for this reason they named two judges in Castile,
and when one went to the court, that the other might defend the land.

Who were these judges?
One was Nuño Rasura and the other Laín Calvo.
And why did they call Nuño Rasura by this name?
Because he took from Castile equal measures of wheat,
and offered them to St James so that he would help them against the Moors.]

In direct comparison to the passage from the *Liber regum*, this one lacks its subordinated clauses. For example, 'E pues acordoron se & eslieron dos iudices porque s' cabdellassen d'estos dos iudices' is expressed 'E porque los castellanos ivan a cortes al rey de León con fijas e mugieres, / por esta razón fizieron en Castilla dos alcaldes, / e quando fuesse el uno a la corte, que'l otro manparasse la tierra,' such that the subordinated clause of the first, 'so that they might be led by these two judges,' is expressed as 'And because ... / for this reason ... / and when one went to the court, / that the other might defend the land.' There is of course some subordination understood in the final clause, but the imperfect subjunctive verb (*manparasse*) is more of an echo of the past-tense verb that precedes it (*fuesse*) than part of a subordinated clause.[8] The rest of the passage is composed of parallel structures and the repetition of *e(t)*, which is employed four times to initiate clauses, and twice as a simple coordinating conjunction.

In sum, the similarity of content helps clarify a difference of degrees in the syntax of the two passages. Both are structured by the repetition of *e(t)*, a coordinating conjunction that allows the narrator to string together his ideas one clause at a time. In order to employ a more complex syntactic structure, the narrator would be forced to think through two clauses, which requires more reflection and is not likely to occur in the initial oral composition.[9] This subordinating strategy does occur three times in the brief passage from the *Liber regum* and not at all in the *Mocedades* passage, suggesting that while both were composed orally, the *Liber regum* received subsequent editing.

Because this use of *e(t)* as a structuring device finds a parallel in the spontaneous speech observed in Chafe's subjects (Chafe 1980, 30; 1987, 17), we may safely surmise that it represents oral discourse. Further confirmation is obtained by way of comparison with Homeric poetry, where the particle *dé* [and] is referred to as a 'step-over conjunction,' because of its role in marking steps in Homeric discourse. In marking steps, *dé* introduces new information as the narrator progresses from one focus of consciousness to another (Bakker 1997, 62–3). Coordination is the function of the particle *kaí*, also translated as *and*, and which Bakker terms the particle of inclusion, as opposed to *dé*, the particle of progression. *Kaí* is 'the particle used to coordinate two elements into a single idea that may (but need not) be expressed as one intonation unit' (71).

From the examples and descriptions that Bakker provides, *kaí* seems to function in Homeric Greek in the same way as *e(t)* in Old Spanish, modern Spanish *y*, as a coordinating conjunction. Yet in the *Mocedades*, as well as in the *Liber regum*, *e(t)* also can be understood as marking narrative progression. Although previous editors of the *Mocedades* have not noted the use of *e(t)* in the marking of narrative progression, it seems to fulfil that function. If we take another look at the passage cited from the *Mocedades*, the examples of *e(t)* can be seen to function as particles of progression as well as particles of inclusion. For this purpose the lines will be distributed so as to acknowledge instances of marking the steps of the narrative:

a) E porque los castellanos ivan a cortes,
b) al rey de León,
c) con fijas e mugieres,
d) por esta razón fizieron en Castilla dos alcaldes,
e) e quando fuesse el uno a la corte,
f) que'l otro manparasse la tierra.
g) ¿Quáles fueron estos alcaldes?
h) El uno fue Nuño Rasura
i) e el otro Laín Calvo.
j) ¿E por qué dixieron Nuño Rasura este nonbre?
k) Porque cogió de Castilla señas eminas de pan,
l) e fizo voto a Santiago,
m) que les ayudasse contra los moros.

If we follow Chafe's elucidation of the cognitive processes involved in spontaneous speech, we can represent this passage as composed of thirteen distinct focuses of consciousness, each one expressed as a single idea unit, with each focus providing details different enough from the previously articulated focus to be perceived as a separate event. As the narrator moves from one focus of consciousness to another, he does so in something similar to steps, each one moving the narration forward. In this process the particle *e(t)* is employed four times as a marker of narrative progression (a, e, j, l) and twice to coordinate ideas that form part of the same focus of consciousness (c, i). There exists, then, a double function for *e(t)*, employed here as a particle of progression and of inclusion, reminiscent of the two Homeric particles discussed by Bakker, *dé* and *kaí*.

At first glance the narrator seems to be moving forward sequentially by describing actions and their actors as he constructs the early history of Castile. But a closer look reveals something quite different. The first six foci seem to elaborate on the election of the two judges or captains who governed Castile (*a–f*), related in *d*.[10] But in the three foci before the election is related, the narrator anticipates the need for background information, provided in *a–c*. Background information is again supplied in the two foci following the statement on the election (*e, f*), suggesting that the narrator has determined that the election of two judges requires additional explanation. The narration then proceeds to reactivate the idea of two judges by asking their names in *g*, in order to identify them in *h* and *i* (Nuño Rasura and Laín Calvo). More detail is then offered on Nuño Rasura (*k, l, m*), one of the two judges, after the narrator asks in *j* why he was given this name. In sum, a good deal of background information accompanies the few simple facts provided in the construction of this passage from the narration of the early history of Castile.

The narrator seems to sense that without this information his narration would make little sense, or hold little interest for the audience. Its focal point is the identification of the two Castilian governors, Nuño Rasura and Laín Calvo, whom he names and identifies, and through them and their offspring he eventually narrates the deeds of their descendants, King Fernando I, descended from Nuño Rasura, and Rodrigo Díaz, descended form Laín Calvo. But his narration is not a genealogy; it is a story filled with curious details. By way of contrast, the *Liber regum* takes the narration directly from Nuño Rasura and Laín Calvo to the emperor of Castile, Alfonso VII (1126–57), great-grandson of King Fernando I, and Rodrigo Díaz, the Cid Campeador, without the enhancements to make it a story. This is not a story; it is a chronicle interested only in establishing an early genealogy for the heroes of Spain. There is nothing to hold the interest of an audience; therefore there can be no audience. This distinction suggests that the *Liber regum* was composed for preservation in writing, while the *Mocedades* was composed with the enjoyment of an audience, and perhaps also their edification, in mind.

One of the more interesting elements of the *Moceedades* are the passages dealing directly with the history of the diocese of Palencia, since they are not present in any of the chronicles that narrate Rodrigo's youth (Deyermond 1969, 154). In fact, the presence of these passages marks the extant *Mocedades* as 'the work of a learned author who wished to help the diocese of Palencia at a critical moment in its history' (Deyermond 1969, 195), a concept revisited in the light of later scholarship and reiterated (1999, 11). But not all scholars are willing to classify the entire poem based on the provenance of 'the 126 lines dealing with the affairs of the diocese' (Montgomery 1984a, 1). Even so, in these references Deyermond finds 'a familiarity with documents and their preparation that would be natural in a lawyer or administrator, but would be grounds for a considerable surprise if the poet were a lay, popular *juglar*' (1969, 79). Deyermond is here referring to the detail of the physical description of documents, the mention of a hanging seal, and the appreciation for the quality of a *signum*.

This is an interesting observation and deserves a brief reconsideration. Let us turn to a passage that contains one of the references mentioned by Deyermond: for him v. 168 'con mio signo otorgado' (1969, 79), here v. 219. It is of special interest to us because it also contains a description of the boundaries of the land privileged for the diocese of Palencia. To a cleric motivated to write the foundational history of the Palencia diocese, its specific boundaries would be important to establish.

The passage begins with the escape of Archbishop Miro of Toledo from the Moors who have conquered the city. Miro comes upon his nephew Bernardo, who is keeping the holy shrine of Saint Antolin Martyr. Bernardo leaves the shrine to his uncle, who then proceeds to ask King Sancho to grant him the shrine and Palencia, where he can lead a holy life as a hermit. What follows is King Sancho's response, which includes a description of the privilege he grants to Miro:

> Commo lo yo conpré del conde don Pedro, franco dólo de grado.
> E fagan un previllegio con mio signo otorgado,
> de la Huerta del Campo, do es Oter Redondo llamado,
> con las cuestas del Atalaya e de los Cascajares del Bravo,
> e de la otra parte, las cuestas commo van a Valroçiado. (vv. 218–22)[11]

> [Since I bought it from Count don Pedro, I gladly give it freely.
> And have them draw up a deed granted with my seal,
> from Huerta del Campo, where it is called Oter Redondo,
> including the Atalaya hills and the Cascajares del Bravo,
> and on the other side, the hills that go up to Valrociado.]

The privilege is a simple one, laying out the territorial boundaries of what eventually would constitute a diocese. The description is consistent with the description of the land around Palencia that precedes it in the poem as open and unpopulated: 'Bravo era el val de Palençia, que non avía y poblado, / sinon do llaman Santa María la Antigua, do morava el conde lozano' (vv. 155–6) [Wild was the vale of Palenica, for there was no settlement there, / except for where they call Santa María La Antigua, where the gallant count lived] (vv. 155–6).

In formulating his arguments for clerical authorship of the poem, Deyermond examined the authentic foundation privilege granted by Sancho el Mayor in 1035 A.D. He points out that its recreation in the poem 'gives a fair picture of the spirit as well as the actual provisions of the original' (Deyermond 1969, 100). The details are not all present, and some differ, but this is because the poet was writing for the widest possible audience, which would be 'bewildered and bored by a lengthy recapitulation of the terms of the document' (100). He also notes the discrepancy between the list of places under the Bishop's temporal jurisdiction according to the privilege and the description of the territory in the *Mocedades* (cited above). This discrepancy suggests that the poet did not have the document in front of him as he wrote, but that he was 'clearly familiar with it' (Deyermond 1969, 101).

In order to clarify, let us look at the list of places in the orginal document, which reads as follows:

Santam Mariam de Fusellis, com suis Villis, & suis Decanijs, vel suis terminis antiquis: Sanctum Jacobum, cum suis terminis antiquis, Sanctam Crucem, Sanctam Mariam de Villa Abarca, Villam Iouenales, Patellam, Pozos, Villam Godel, Villam Momiam, cum illarum terminis antiquis, Villam Letificus, Buardo, Campum rotundum, Alvam, cum illorum, & illarum terminis suis. (Deyermond 1969, 100–1n41)[12]

The focus of this privilege on established parishes and towns is quite different from the description in the *Mocedades* of territorial boundaries, in consonance with its overall portrayal of Palencia as a vast, unpopulated vale. Of course, the poem is projecting back some three hundred years to the time of King Sancho el Mayor (d. 1035), and unless the narrator had direct knowledge of the original document, he might well believe that Palencia was not yet settled.

From this brief comparison of the two descriptions, it seems that the original document had no influence at all in the representation of the privilege in the *Mocedades*. The reference in the poem to Santa María la Antigua as the residence of count Pedro de Campó, the original holder of the title to the Palencia lands, may be the same place as either Santam Mariam de Fusellis or Sanctam Mariam de Villa Abarca in the original privilege, but even that is not readily apparent. More importantly it seems, the intention of the original privilege was to identify the existing parishes and their holdings that were to come under the jurisdiction of the diocese of Palencia, while the privilege in the *Mocedades* means to suggest that there were no legal establishments transferred in the creation of the diocese, just unoccupied lands given freely by the king to the Church.

Later in the poem, Bishop Miro dies and King Fernando grants the bishopric to Bernardo. Bernardo takes the privilege to Rome, has it confirmed, and returns to Spain, where King Fernando re-confirms the exemptions that King Sancho had granted. This passage includes a second description of the boundaries of the diocese in lines 340–4:

> Allí llegó de Palençia el mandado que era muerto el obispo Miro.
> E dio el obispado a Bernardo,
> e enbió1' quel' confirmase a Roma,
> e vino muy buen perlado.
> E otorgó sus libertades que el rey Sancho Avarca avía dado,
> desde la Huerta del Topo fasta do es La Quintanilla con todo,
> fasta Castiel Redondo, do es Magaz llamado,
> detrás de las Cuestas de los Cascajares, do es Santo Thomé llamado,
> fasta las otras cuestas que llaman Val Royado,
> do llaman Val de Pero, ca non era poblado.
> Mandó en los previllejos poner signo el buen rey don Fernando. (vv. 335–45)

> [From Palencia the news arrived there that bishop Miro was dead.
> And he gave the bishopric to Bernardo,
> and he sent him to Rome to be confirmed,
> and he returned a very fine prelate.
> And he reconfirmed the grants that king Sancho Abarca had given,
> from Huerta del Topo up to Quintanilla and its surroundings,
> up to Castiel Redondo, where it is called Magaz,
> from the other side of the Cascajares hills, where it is called Santo Tomé,
> up to the other hills that are called Val Royado,
> where it's called Val de Pero, which was not settled.
> The good king don Fernando ordered his seal put on the grants.]

In comparing the two descriptions from the poem it seems unlikely that the narrator is being guided by a written source. They are similar, but 'la Huerta del Campo' [the fertile plain of the countryside] (v. 220), becomes 'la Huerta del Topo' [the fertile plain of the mole] (340); 'Oter Redondo'

[Round Knoll] (220) becomes 'Castiel Redondo' [Round Castle] (341); 'las cuestas del Atalaya' [the Lookout hills] and the 'cascajares del Bravo' [The gravel banks of the Bravo (river)] (221) become 'las Cuestas de los Cascajares' [The hills of the Gravel Banks] (342). Both descriptions finish with the same boundary, although written differently, 'las cuestas commo van a Valroçiado' (222), and 'las otras cuestas que llaman Val Royado' (343), suggesting that it was probably written from dictation, in which case the spelling represents two attempts to approximate the same sound, the ç (voiceless dental fricated) and the y (voiceless prepalatal fricative).

The other differences noted above are also not likely to have occurred while a poem was composed in writing. The process of writing the poem would have allowed the poet to check for accuracy, especially in the description of lands so dear to the clerics of Palencia. In the second description, there are additional markers that seem to function as clarification for the more general description of the first, as if the places described are not specific enough and require more detail. For example, 'la Huerta del Campo' (220), probably a geographic term, becomes 'la Huerta del Topo fasta do es la Quintanilla con todo' (340), which seems to be a reference to the same place with the additional marker of a villa and its surroundings. 'Oter Redondo' (220) becomes 'Castiel Redondo, do es Magaz llamado' (341). The first seems to correspond closely to the Latin 'Campum rotundum' of the original privilege, probably a round outcropping of some sort. In 'Castiel Redondo' it takes on the meaning of a man-made structure, with the added reference to what looks like a town, 'Magaz' (341). In line 342 'Cuestas' and 'Cascajares,' which are two distinct landmarks in 221, are joined, which at best means they refer to a different place altogether, or no place at all, with an additional reference to the town or parish of Santo Thomé (342).

Overall the second description of the privilege seems to identify the same natural landmarks as the first, but then adds to each one a man-made structure or landmark. In order to see this more clearly, let us look first at the landmarks alone:

de la Huerta del Campo, do es Oter Redondo llamado,
con las cuestas del Atalaya e de los Cascajares del Bravo,
e de la otra parte, las cuestas commo van a Valroçiado (vv. 220–2)

desde la Huerta del Topo, (341) fasta Castiel Redondo,
detrás de las Cuestas de los Cascajares,
fasta las otras cuestas que llaman Val Royado, (vv. 340–3)

Seen this way, the landmarks are similar enough, yet the differences between them cannot be accounted for as simply copyist error. 'Campo' becomes 'Topo,' which may be attributed to copyist error, but 'Oter' becomes 'Castiel,' which is a more meaningful change, suggesting a castle or other structure constructed on the knoll. The change that is clearly of another magnitude is the re-articulation of line 221 in line 342, because it transforms the first half of the line, making it another reference altogether:

> 221: con las cuestas del Atalaya e de los Cascajares del Bravo,
> 342: detrás de las Cuestas de los Cascajares, do es Santo Thomé llamado,

The different emphasis and the misconstrued landmarks of the second description seem to identify an entirely different place. This change most likely reflects intervention in a previously written text, an alteration made in order to accommodate new points of reference, more specific than the first. If so, the intervening hand would have removed 'del Atalaya' and 'del Bravo' from the description and added 'do es Santo Thomé llamado.' The resulting landmark, 'las Cuestas de los Cascajares' [the hills of the gravel banks or beds] is new, clearly not the same place as 'the Lookout hills' and 'the gravel banks of the Bravo [river].' In fact, the references to the natural landmarks have been altered beyond recognition, and the new references are all man-made structures. The result is a new emphasis on place names and a disregard for the natural landmarks of the first description of the privilege.

This change in emphasis becomes even more apparent when we look at the place names that have been added to the second description of the privilege. There are references to villas (probably a farm with additional buildings for dependents) and towns, as in a small grouping of villas (La Quintanilla), two towns (Magaz and Santo Thomé) or a parish (Santo Thomé), and a vale (Val de Pero 'Peter's Vale'), as listed below:

> 340: fasta do es La Quintanilla con todo,
> 341: do es Magaz llamado,
> 342: do es Santo Thomé llamado
> 344: do llaman Val de Pero, ca non era poblado.

These additions were made with more or less trauma to pre-existing verses, as noted above regarding line 342. In the final instance an entirely new verse was added, 'do llaman Val de Pero, ca non era poblado' (344). Here we have the name of one valley or vale replacing another:

fasta las otras cuestas que llaman Val Royado,
do llaman Val de Pero, ca non era poblado. (vv. 343–4)

This analysis has shown that in the first description of the privilege in
the *Mocedades* the emphasis was on natural landmarks, giving the im-
pression that no towns were involved in the granting of the privilege by
King Sancho to the church at Palencia. This is in contrast to the original
privilege in Latin, which clearly identifies entire parishes as well as
towns and villas in its description of the Palencia diocese. In the poem's
second description the landmarks are minimized in order to give
greater prominence to towns and a parish as identifiers of boundaries.
This notable change in emphasis between the first and the second descriptions most likely reveals two distinct moments in the elaboration
of the extant manuscript.

In either case, the description of the diocesan boundaries as a vast
and unpopulated land is in sharp contrast to the original privilege in
Latin, which we may suppose reflects the authentic landscape of the
time, one populated by well-defined parishes and towns, and which
must have been approved by the interested clerics. The first privilege in
the *Mocedades* is then demonstrably not clerical in this strict sense at
least, in that it contradicts a document that is known to be clerical. It
may also reflect a popular, or non-learned, notion of how boundaries
are understood. Another consideration is that its desire to portray the
diocesan boundaries as unpopulated lands may reflect an effort to dis-
courage or discredit land claims against the diocese. If so, then the
second privilege in the *Mocedades* undermines somewhat that effort by
diminishing the importance of the natural landmarks and adding the
names of towns and a parish for better specificity. The return to popula-
tion centres as a way to better identify the boundaries of the diocese
also suggests that this second hand was clerical and that the intervention was made over a pre-existing traditional narrative, all of which is in
consonance with earlier findings on the nature of the alterations in the
Mocedades manuscript (Montgomery 1984a, 12–14; Webber 1980, 210–
11; Funes 2004, xxix–xxxiv).

Finally, the second privilege, marked as it is by clerical intervention,
is in the midst of a passage of oral composition. The lines immediately
preceding the description of the privilege reveal little that is poetic;
they seem at best to be simple enunications of unadorned speech:

Allí llegó de Palençia el mandado que era muerto el obispo Miro.
E dio el obispado a Bernardo,

e enbiól' quel' confirmase a Roma,
e vino muy buen perlado.
E otorgó sus libertades que el rey Sancho Avarca avía dado (vv. 335–9)

The distribution of these lines is open to debate, but the major organizational principle is not assonance at the end of the line, but rather the use of *e(t)* at the beginning. This structuring device is found in a number of passages in the poem and is common in spontaneous speech and in Homeric poetry, as indicated earlier. In each of the five instances of its use here, *e(t)* is marking steps in the narration, introducing new information as the narrator progresses from one focus of consciousness to another. In this formulation there is no need to subordinate clauses, as one line follows another in sequence, making all statements of equal value, linked only paratactically. As established earlier, this structuring principle is inherent in orally composed narration, not of learned poetry or prose, which typically integrates ideas through syntactic subordination.

The observations made here all point to a *Mocedades* narrative that manifests essential charactersitics of oral discourse, although in some passages there is also evidence of later learned intervention. The link between the expressive traits of the poem and similar expression in the Homeric poems and in the speech subjects of the linguist Wallace Chafe provides additional grounds for asserting that oral composition was employed in the poem's initial placement on parchment. Later intervention by a learned chronicler has also been confirmed. In summary, the extant *Mocedades* manuscript exhibits signs of oral and written composition, although the evidence for written composition is limited to interventions made on a pre-existent text, which are largely responsible for its least poetic tendencies. For the learned cleric, the poem seems to have lost its meaning, and like the great warrior it celebrates, to have lost its place among men who no longer share its values.

Conclusion

The texts of thirteenth-century Spain are varied in language and in function. Yet the Latin texts of the learned clerics and the vernacular epic narratives have more in common than is generally acknowledged, especially in their use of speech in the compositional process. Once composed, however, the learned texts passed through additional stages of editorial reworking that mask their link to an initial oral composition. Not so for the epic poems that are spoken in the language of the poet, scribe, and audience. These narratives retain many of the features of spoken discourse because they are composed in a fashion that binds expression to form, which makes them less malleable in later hands.

There is of course notable clerical influence in the vernacular epic, but this tells us very little about its mode of composition. Medieval clerics of all stripes dictated their texts orally to scribes writing on wax tablets. This was common practice, as we saw in the case of Santo Martino de León, who wrote on wax tablets while simultaneously dictating to scribes, and eventually supervised the transfer of all that was taken down onto parchment. Yet the finished copies of their texts bear little resemblance to spoken discourse, demonstrating that the initial dictation was only the first stage in the production of a learned text.

The epic poems we have studied here – the *Cid*, the *Fernán González*, and the *Mocedades* – all display expressive features long associated with narratives performed orally. Their paratactic structure, end-rhyme, and abundant use of formulaic language are elements familiar to us in the many guises of performance poetry, be it medieval, Homeric, or South Slavic. More importantly, what we have been able to show here is that these poems exhibit many of the same expressive characteristics as the spontaneous speech of the modern-day subjects of Wallace Chafe's linguistic studies.

In both cases their expression is a response to the cognitive constraints that govern the oral narration of thoughts and action, either those portrayed in the Pear Film, or of heroic deeds attributed to the legendary Castilian warriors in their thirteenth-century recreations. The similarities in their expression are attributable to the fact that they are being produced before an expectant audience, with decisions about phrasing, emphasis, and effectiveness made in real time through a symbiotic relationship between speaker and listener.

In the textual analysis of these epic poems, the awareness of the cognitive constraints operating on the poet as he narrates his story, and the analysis of the cognitively based expression he deploys as his narrative moves forward, have allowed us to link expression in the text to cognition in the poet's mind as he shifts focus from narration to commentary, from concrete idea to abstraction, from the concrete actions of his protagonist to comparisons with universals. This new understanding of the complex dynamic involved in the oral production of epic poetry has allowed us to redefine the function of some of the expressive features of these works, to understand them less as stylistic choices or conscious narrative strategies and more as mechanisms that allow the narrator to maintain more than one train of thought while at the same time moving the story forward.

I believe that the question of the mode of composition of these texts has been answered here. These poems were produced orally, even though clerics played a role in their production, whether in their initial composition or in a more limited way, in their overall design and in the process of their placement onto parchment. They are speech-based narratives with culturally determined subjects and expressions, crafted by tradition and individual genius, not exactly the spontaneous speech of Chafe's subjects, but a kind of specialized speech shared by the poets of the time, so perfect in its functionality that it continues to move us today. This means that the manuscript texts we have are transcriptions of poems that were spoken by the poets themselves, as if before an audience of their contemporaries who spoke their language and shared their values. Unlike the Latin and other learned texts of the time, there is essentially no mediation between the speakers of these epic poems and today's readers. This immediacy is the source of their power over us and the justification for their unique status in the literature of medieval Spain.

Notes

Introduction

1 Alfonso X's *Estoria de España* (ca 1284) makes reference to some thirteen
   epic narratives, some of which are included in their entirety. In addition, a
   brief passage of 100 verses, known as the *Roncesvalles* fragment, may be an
   epic passage or a ballad (see edition in Gómez Redondo 1996, 139–45).
   Alan Deyermond accounts for twenty-nine traditional Spanish epic
   narratives that are now lost to us (1995, 54–137). Colin Smith (1984)
   provides an interesting itinerary of the vicissitudes suffered by the epic
   and other lost literature of medieval Spain.
2 Lucas (Bishop) of Túy's *Chronicon mundi* (1236) and Archbishop (of Toledo)
   Rodrigo Ximénez de Rada's *De rebus Hispanie* (1243) are mentioned
   frequently as primary sources in Alfonso's *Estoria de España*.
3 On the inclusion of oral epic in Alfonsine chronicles see Menéndez Pidal
   (1951, 45–69). See also the interesting textual examples of a thirteenth-
   century chronicler's ruminations on the veracity of epic tales in Fradejas
   Lebrero (1991, 31–51, esp. 36–8).
4 The *Crónica de veinte reyes* (ca 1282–4), also known as the *Versión crítica de
   la Estoria de España* for its clearly focused historiographical perspective
   evidenced through a critical attitude toward sources (Fernández Ordóñez
   1992, 11–25, esp. 25), includes a number of commentaries by the narrator
   of the history in favour of written sources when these clash with the
   version of events presented by oral sources, as evidenced in the following
   citation: 'Mas como quier que en el cantar del rrey don Sancho diga que
   luego fue sobrel rrey don García, fallamos en las estorias verdaderas que
   cuenta y el arçobispo don Rodrigo, e don Lucas de Tuy, e don pero

Marques, cardenal de Santiago, que ovieron sabor de escudriñar las estorias por contar verdaderamente la estoria d'España, que sobre el rrey don Alfonso fue luego que estaua en comedio, e esta fue la verdat. Mas porque vos non [sic] queremos contar aquí conplidamente toda la estoria del rrey don Sancho, asy commo la cuentan los juglares, dexaremos aquí de contarla asy commo la cuenta el arçobispo e los otros sabios, ca después lo contaremos adelante bien e compidamente, e deziruos hemos del rrey don Sancho y del rrey don García.' [But even though in the epic poem of King don Sancho it says that he first attacked King don García, we find in the true histories related by Archbishop don Rodrigo, and don Lucas de Tuy, and don Pero Marques, Cardinal of Santiago, who took it upon themselves to examine the histories in order to relate truthfully the history of Spain, that he first attacked King don Alfonso who was in the middle, and this was the truth. But because we do not [sic] want to tell you here fully the whole story of King don Sancho, the way the minstrels tell it, we will stop telling it as the Archbishop and the other learned men tell it, and later we will take it up again well and fully, and we will tell you about king don Sancho and king don García.] (Libro IX, cap. IIII°; *Crónica de veinte reyes* 1991, 183). Most noteworthy for this study is the recognition of the dissemination of an epic poem (*cantar*) by minstrels (*juglares*).

5 I use the term 'poet' here to represent my conception of the Spanish *juglar* as a composer and performer of the medieval Spanish epic, in spite of the fact that in the minds of many it links inexorably to text. As a translation of *juglar*, 'minstrel' is an acceptable term, comparable in function to the French 'jongleur.' Lord's term 'singer' is appropriate for the Yugoslav *guslar*, as it emphasizes the performance of their poems in a sing-song style.

6 A few of these deeds are also narrated in the Latin *Historia Roderici*, dated by some specialists as early as 1110, only eleven years after the Cid's historical death in 1099.

7 Salvador Martínez reviews the scant documentation on the life of Fernán González and situates the most active period of his warrior activity from 947 to 948 (1991, 9–16).

8 *Juglares* are identified in the thirteenth-century Alfonsine *Estoria de España* as saying or speaking their narratives, but there is no documental evidence to determine how their narratives were composed or recorded (Menéndez Pidal 1924, 368–9).

9 This process is described in detail in Clanchy (1979, esp. 177–82, 216–18), and examples are well documented in Stock (1983, 409) and Mary Carruthers (1990, 6), reviewed in Bailey 2003 (256).

1. The Critical Response to Oral Composition

1 Thomas Montgomery brings to our attention an archaic formal language preserved in the *Cid* that points to a 'habit of oral composition latent in the poem's background' (1998, 111). However, 'tradition-based epic texts such as the *Poema del Cid* stand at the juncture of orality – language heard – and literacy – language seen and accordingly preserved,' and Montgomery sees the possible influence of writing in the bold measures the poet has taken 'to bend his story to convey messages that are of his time rather than inherited with the tradition,' but does not attempt to answer 'whether the *Cid* has undergone such revisions with the aid of the tool of writing' (150). Alan Deyermond assumes a long period of oral composition for the Spanish epic, and the probable memorization of much of the *Cid* in its extant form (1995, 52). John S. Miletich distinguishes 'hemistichs in which a similar idea recurs from those in which there is no such recurrence' (1981, 189) as a tool for determining the degree of oral or literate composition of a text, which leads him to conclude that 'the *Poema de mio Cid* is a text composed in writing in which oral tradition has to some extent played a part, and that it was destined for oral diffusion' (194). Irene Zaderenko postulates that the entire poem was composed in writing, although some sources may have been oral (1998, 88, 126, 153, 170, 188, 191–2).

2 There is no serious questioning of the genesis of the Spanish epic by Menéndez Pidal and therefore no clear statement on epic composition. He simply assumes that the poem is written and makes a number of indirect statements to that effect. In these statements he seems to be simply stating what for him is obvious. For instance, the proof that the story of the Moorish Princess Zaida is a written epic narrative lies in the many details proffered; these are 'pormenores profusos que las tradiciones orales son incapaces de conservar' [profuse details that oral traditions are incapable of preserving]; such detail 'tenía que conservarse en un relato escrito' [must have been preserved in a written account] (1951, 55–6). Menéndez Pidal refers to the written epic in the context of its recitation by *juglares* [minstrels], specifying that we cannot speak of minstrels, because we do not know the names of any of them; we must speak of 'obras de carácter juglaresco' [works characteristic of minstrels]: 'A los autores de éstas llamaremos juglares, sin tener seguridad de que lo fuesen, es decir, sin saber si hacían de la recitación de los poemas un oficio o modo de vivir, o si eran hombres de otra posición social, que escribían para abastecer la recitación pública de los que a esta profesión se dedicaban' [We'll call the authors of these poems minstrels without knowing for sure if that is what

they were, which is to say, without knowing if they made a living from the recitation of their poems, or if they were men of another social position who wrote to supply the public recitation of those who dedicated themselves to this profession] (1945, 190 [1924, 313]). In a clarification of what he means by *juglares*, Menéndez Pidal states: 'al hablar de "juglares" en el siglo XII, no quiero decir sino "poetas que escriben para legos," pero no "poetas indoctos," desconocedores de la literatura latina' [when speaking of minstrels in the twelfth century, I mean to say nothing other than poets who write for the laity, but not uncultured poets, ignorant of Latin literature]. Also, 'El juglar del Cid (entiéndase juglar docto y altísimo poeta) escribe para gentes que saben ...' [The minstrel of the *Cid* (meaning a learned poet of the highest order) writes for people who know ...] (Menéndez Pidal 1945, 80, 92). In his later work (*En torno*), Menéndez Pidal continues to assume a written text for the *Cid* and even goes so far as to distinguish two distinct styles and emphases in the first and second halves of the poem. Here again, the emphasis lies not in the fact that the poem is written, but on the clarification of its date of composition: 'La fecha en que escribió este poeta de Gormaz debió ser a raíz de la muerte del héroe' [The date when this poet from Gormaz wrote must have been soon after the death of the hero]; and again: 'Cuando el poeta de Gormaz escribe' [When the poet from Gormaz writes] (1963, 146). Finally, while speaking of the poem's swift success, and in reference to the two poets he believed composed what he had come to understand as two parts of the work, he states that 'escribían fuera de la Vieja Castilla' [They wrote while away from Old Castile' (1963, 218).

3 Adam Parry, the son of Milman Parry, collected, edited, translated into English when necessary, and published all of his father's writings, including the two theses published for his doctoral program at the University of Paris in 1928. All citations of Milman Parry's work are from Adam Parry (1971).

4 Deyermond was a plenary speaker at the 41st International Congress on Medieval Studies at Western Michigan University (Kalamazoo), speaking on 'Historical Fictions in Medieval Castile' (6 May 2006).

5 The full quotation follows: 'Although we cannot entirely exclude the idea of a cleric who was also a *juglar* and could compose orally (cf. *BHS*, xlii, 7), we have no evidence that would justify such an assumption in this case, and composition in writing is much more likely. Clerics could be *juglares*, as we see from a thirteenth-century miniature reproduced by Menéndez Pidal (*Poesía juglaresca*, facing p. 332), but it is very doubtful whether this would apply to diocesan administrators' (Deyermond 1969, 201n19).

6 The reference to Lord in the quotation is from the original.

7 I employ the Spanish translation of Zumthor's work, *La lettre et la voix 1987 (La letra y la voz)*, because it is familiar to Hispano-medievalists.

8 The criticism continues, as Foley points out the 'tautology entailed in prescribing "quality" [in Deyermond's formulation 'wealth of patterns'] as equivalent to what one perceives as the (literary) merit of Homeric poems. Such a parochial concept simply leaves no room for other kinds of excellence, just as it unnaturally restricts the possible range of Homer's own excellence' (Foley 1999, 41).

2. Learned Culture

1 In all instances in which an original and a translation are furnished, the translation is mine.

2 Passage from *Poema de Santa Oria*, Gonzalo de Berceo.

3 In crafting my translation of the poem, I have consulted and benefited from the translation by Anthony Lappin (2000).

4 There is no explicit parallel between Saint Eugenia and Oria in the narration, but Oria does take inspiration from Eugenia, a virgin martyr. James F. Burke asserts that Berceo shapes the parallel in order to emphasize that 'the ascetic virgin is a martyr' (1973, 300).

5 Narrated in chapters 96–102 of the *Historia Silense*, provided in English translation in Barton and Fletcher (2000, 56–60).

6 The tomb carries an inscription that identifies the two bodies it holds: 'Hunc quem cernjs lapidem scultum sacra tegit menbra Beata. simul auria uirgo cum matre amunna quiescunt femina. Et quja pro christo artham duxerunt ujtam symul cum eo. meruerunt coronari. jn gloria' (Walsh 1972, 302).

7 Details from the narrative of the life of Saint Eugenia, *Vita Sanctae Eugeniae*, have been identified in Oria's narrative, although in this case the parallels are attributed to Berceo, as the author of the text (Walsh 1972). The vision of Bishop Alvito does not bring to mind any particular text, although a parallel may be found in the story of Balaam's donkey, in which Balaam strikes his donkey three times with his staff before God gives the power of speech to the donkey, allowing Balaam to finally see the angel of Yahweh standing on the road before him with his sword drawn to block his way (Numbers 22:22–35). The narrator also has trouble identifying a relevant text, as indicated by his comment that the bishop recited a psalm, 'I know not which.'

8 The first mention of this testimony, along with other interesting examples, is found in a recent article arguing for the oral composition of the *Cid* (Duggan 2005, 51–7).

9 Saint Isidore is the same religious community that produced the *Translatio Sancti Isidori.*

10 Martin commenced writing his *opera* in 1185.

11 In Martin's text it is the visionary who lights up after eating the scroll, whereas in Ezekiel and John it is God who appears to the prophet as a 'brilliance, like amber, like fire … like fire, giving a brilliance all around' (Ezekiel 1:27–8). In John's text God is seated on a throne from which came 'flashes of lightning' (Revelation 4:5).

12 The Latin text is from chapter 63 of the facsimile edition of chapters 52–75 of the *Liber Miraculis de Sancti Isidori,* by Lucas de Tuy, which is referred to as *Liber de Vita et Miraculis Sancti Martini* (Viñayo 1984, 7–48). The resolution of the shorthand and the translation are mine. The Castilian translation included in the volume is from the sixteenth century and takes liberties with the original, which make it unsuitable for my purposes.

13 As in the following description of *De judiciis astrologiae*: 'Por encargo de Alfonso se tradujo el libro del árabe; según técnica tradicional Judá ben Mosé leía el texto arábigo y daba de palabra su traducción al vulgar; Álvaro, oída esa traducción al vulgar, dictaba a un escriba la versión latina' [As ordered by Alfonso the book was translated from the Arabic; in accordance with traditional methods Judá ben Mosé read the Arabic text and spoke his translation in the vulgar tongue; Álvaro, hearing the translation to the vulgar tongue, dictated to a scribe the Latin version] (G. Menéndez Pidal 1951, 366).

14 Quien escrivió este libro dél' Dios paraíso, amen.
Per Abbat le escrivió en el mes de mayo (*Cid*, vv. 3731–2) [Who wrote down this book, may God give him Paradise, amen. Per Abbat wrote it down in the month of May]. Rene Pellen provides more detail on the use of the terms *escribir* and *libro* (Pellen 1998, 185 and 187–8 respectively).

15 As Duggan points out, 'If a Spanish version of the *Song of Roland* circulated in this early period, French versions were surely sung even earlier (2006, 66–7).

16 Lucas is also the author of the *Liber de Miraculis Sancti Isidori,* examined earlier.

17 I am translating *histrionum* (histrio -onis), 'actor, dramatic artist,' as 'jongleur,' because that seems to be how it is used here.

18 These events are narrated in chapters 619 and 623 of the *Estoria de España* (Menéndez Pidal 1955, 352–7). The title given to Alfonso's history by Menéndez Pidal is *Primera crónica general de España.* It has since fallen out of favour, and scholars prefer to refer to the work as *Estoria de España.* Alfonso may have begun gathering materials for his history as early as

1270, and it is thought to have been completed by 1289, during the reign of his son Sancho IV (1284–95).

19 Citations from the poem are from the edition of Juan Gil (1990).

20 Line 28 in Gil's text reads '<m>ore uirorum,' which makes little sense, and in this rendering I follow Montaner and Escobar (2001, 200).

21 Among the more recent proponents of an early date for the *Historia* are the historian and English translator of the text, Richard Fletcher, and the editor of the Latin text, Emma Falque, both of whom provide fair and careful arguments for and against their points of view (Barton and Fletcher 2000, 92–8; Falque 1990, 14–21).

22 Proponents of an early dating for the *Historia* consider possible the inclusion of eyewitness accounts in the narration of the Cid's exploits (Barton and Fletcher 2000, 98; Falque 1990, 20).

23 From another perspective, Colin Smith (1983, 143–9) and Irene Zaderenko (1998) consider that the common episodes in the *Cid* and the *Historia* demonstrate that the *Historia* was a source for the *Cid*, from which the author of the poem drew inspiration and material.

24 This is the date assigned to the poem by Salvador Martínez (1975, 121), which corresponds fairly well with the date of composition for the chronicle of between 1147 and 1157, assigned by Barton and Fletcher (2000, 157).

25 The Latin text and a modern Spanish translation of the *Poema de Almería* are included in Salvador Martínez (1975, 22–51). An English translation of the chronicle, including the poem and an introductory study, are included in Barton and Fletcher (2000, 148–263). Antonio Maya Sánchez edits the Latin *Chronica Adefonsi Imperatoris* (Falque, Gil, and Maya 1990, 109–248), and Juan Gil edits the poem, which he titles *Prefatio de Almaria* (Falque, Gil and Maya 1990, 249–67).

3. The *Cantar de Mio Cid*

1 'Deus igitur in hoc opusculo michi sit in auxilium qui me librum hunc componere et in Latinum transferre compulit' (*Disciplina clericalis*, 109), [God, who has compelled me to compose this book and transfer it into Latin, be of aid to me in this little work of mine].

2 Sharp distinctions between oral and written modes of expression are also inappropriate for the modern period, and modern scholars have long questioned absolute distinctions between them. Ruth Finnegan, an anthropologist, provides evidence of a wide array of oral poetry, some of it composed orally but much of it memorized with or without the aid of written texts (Finnegan 1977). Parry and Lord's fieldwork led them to note

briefly the existence of oral poets who had memorized written narratives and presented them orally (Lord 1960, 109). These are not the best poets, but they are practitioners. They also offer the example of a father and son, both literate, who learn and sing their songs orally (109–12).

3 The text and the translation I take from my website (www.laits.utexas .edu/cid), with minor changes made to the translation in order to highlight the expressive aspects under consideration.

4 Deyermond does not employ the term parataxis; instead he refers to the near absence of enjambment (*encabalgamiento*) as characteristic of oral poetry. Either way, both terms (parataxis, absence of enjambment) describe single verses expressing independent units of meaning.

5 These observations regarding the editing of the poem by the Alfonsine chroniclers reflect the work of Nancy Joe Dyer and specific findings of Brian Powell (1983, 87, 91, 97–8).

6 I do not retain Gornall's brackets for indicating scribal abbreviations in the manuscript, which for present purposes are beside the point.

7 For the sake of consistency, I will continue to follow Gornall's use of bold lettering.

8 My numbering coincides with modern editions of the poem in this passage, but I do not always follow their disposition of the verses, which are presented here without additions or corrections to the wording of the manuscript.

9 In his transcription of the episode, Chafe indicates hesitations, variations in pitches, and intonations, which contribute considerably to the effectiveness of the climax. They are not reproduced here in order to maintain the focus on the wording and so facilitate comparisons with the *Cid*.

4. The *Poema de Fernán González*

1 The *Chronica Naierensis* was probably composed in the eighth decade of the twelfth century (ca 1185), most likely by a cleric associated with the Riojan monastery of Santa María la Real de Nájera (Estévez Sola 1995, lxx, lxxix, lxxxix, xciv).

2 Here again, the translations and paraphrasing are mine.

3 It is assumed that the battle being described takes place at Simancas, although the location is not identified in the privilege.

4 On the appropriateness of translating 'Pontificem' as 'bishop,' see Yarza Luaces (1993–4, 749–51).

5 The vernacular prose text is an expansion of the original privilege, much more detailed than the Latin text. It is included in Dutton's study (1967, 11–12).

6 This is certainly the case with a vernacular recreation of the Latin text of the privilege from the fourteenth century. The vernacular text greatly expands the Latin version on which it is based (Dutton 1967, 11–22).

7 The only known author of any of the *mester de clerecía* texts is Gonzalo de Berceo, who composed Marian texts such as the *Milagros de Nuestra Señora*, lives of local Saints such as *Vida de Santo Domingo de Silos, Vida de San Millán de la Cogolla*, and the *Poema de Santa Oria*, among others.

8 The written genesis of *clerecía* poetry is a common critical assumption, seldom stated explicitly. Isabel Uría, for example, reviews a century of scholarship on the diffusion of *clerecía* poetry, but never questions its mode of composition (2000, 134–53).

9 *General estoria*, 1a Parte, lib. XVI, cap. XIV, ms. of the Bibl. Nac. 816, fol. 215a.

10 Juan Manuel identifies the intended audience of a vernacular text in his *Crónica abreviada*: 'los que fazen o mandan fazer algunos libros mayor mente en Romançe que es sennal que se fazen para los legos que no son muy letrados' [those that make or have made some books mainly in Romance, which is a sign that they are made for the laity who are not very learned] (37, lines 7–9).

11 Quotations of the *Fernán González* are from López-Guil (2001). I have used her paleographic transcription of the text (135–225) but have normalized spacing and some distinctions, such as between y / i, j / i, and v / u, as well as adding modern stress accents in order to facilitate reading.

12 The manuscript text reads 'el conde fue tenido, Almozore Golías,' but this makes little sense, while substituting 'David' makes perfect sense (López Guil 2001, 445). Additional support for this emendation is a subsequent reference to David and Goliath in the poem (v. 348c: 'cuentan del rey Davyt que mató a Goljas' [they tell of King David who killed Goliath]).

13 The *Crónica de veinte reyes* (ca 1284) represents the 'versión crítica' [revised version] of Alfonso X's *Estoria de España* (Fernández Ordóñez 1992, 21) The brackets are mine, indicating material not found in the poem, most likely an addition made by the Alfonsine editors, also concerned that their audience appreciate the magnitude of Fernán González's victory. Note also the positive tone of the description of Almanzor, in stark contrast with his depiction in the poem.

5. The *Mocedades de Rodrigo*

1 Leonardo Funes disputes the link between the *Mocedades* and a pan-European initiation myth on the grounds that the similarities between them can be ascribed to the fact that the theme of *enfances* ('youthful deeds') 'tiende por su propia lógica a adoptar la estructura de un mito de

iniciación' (Funes 2004, lviii) [by its own logic tends to adopt the structure of an initiation myth]. I am not sure how to characterize the logic in that statement. Funes points this out in an effort to relate the rebelliousness of Rodrigo to the social circumstances at the time of the poem's composition (Funes 2004, lviii–lix).

2 For more details, see Bailey (2007, 17–18). In the earliest textual rendition of the massacre of the Carolingian rearguard in Spain, the *Nota Emilianense*, the Saracens are the victors (Alonso 1954, 9).

3 A fuller discussion of the dating of *Carmen Campidoctoris* is undertaken in chapter 2. Here again I am following the observations of the editor of the Latin text (Gil 1990, 101), in agreement with Fletcher (1989, 92–3). Objections and a much later date (ca 1181–90) are found in Montaner and Escobar (2001, 130–5).

4 Scholars are not in agreement on the date of composition of this important text, as reported in chapter 2 of this study. For our purposes here, I would like to emphasize that all the suggested dates pre-date the *Mocedades*. As Emma Falque suggests, it is likely that an initial composition was produced early in the twelfth century, only to be modified and added to by later hands (Falque 1990, 20–1).

5 The *Estoria de España* was redacted in two versions, the first between 1270 and 1274, the second between 1282 and 1284 (Fernández Ordóñez 1999, 121). The material cited by Armistead includes both versions, which he refers to as the *Primera crónica general* and the *Crónica de veinte reyes*, respectively.

6 The exact date is not known, but Armistead is in accordance with scholars in general when dating the composition of the *Crónica de Castilla* between 1290 and 1300 (Armistead 2000, 40).

7 In support of his observations, Chafe follows a pre-publication text of Pawley and Syder, which he identifies as 'English Conversational Structures,' in which Pawley and Syder 'find a "strong statistical preference ... for a coordinating, or chaining style of syntax, over a subordinating or integrating style." They suggest that speakers formulate speech "one clause at a time" – in our terms one idea unit at a time – and that "most times a speaker commits himself to a multiclause sentence beginning with a novel clause he takes a gamble. Having composed only a fragment in the first encoding stage, he gambles on being able to formulate in mid-sentence an acceptable continuation and completion." It is easy to string idea units together with *ands*, but trying to do something more complex in spontaneous speech typically leads to awkwardness' (Chafe 1980, 30–1). These ideas are presented with a slightly different emphasis in Pawley and Syder (1983, 202–4).

8 In the case of *fuesse*, the form looks to be imperfect subjunctive, but it is actually the simple perfect tense, as in another instance a few lines later: 'E fuesse para el rey moro Guiben, señor de Madrid' [And he went to the Moorish king Guiben, lord of Madrid] (Bailey 2007, 31, v. 23).

9 Chafe has observed that speakers tend to avoid such integration [the subordinating strategy] or to use only its simpler varieties, and when they attempt something more elaborate they are prone to get into trouble. He surmises that the trouble is caused by an overtaxing of the focus of consciousness, which has limited capacity and duration and cannot easily handle syntactic devices that call for too much commitment of its resources to verbalization processes over too long a period of time (Chafe 1980, 32).

10 In other texts, such as the *Liber regum* cited above, these Castilian leaders are termed *iudices* (modern Spanish *jueces* [judges], with its root in Latin, but here they are *alcaldes* [captain or governor of a city], from the Arabic.

11 This and subsequent citations of text from the *Mocedades* and its translation are from Bailey 2007.

12 The passage lists established parishes and towns, and begins as follows: 'Santa María de Husillos, with her villas, and her deacons, and her old boundaries ...,' followed by additional place names, some of which I am not able to identify.

Works Cited

Aguirre, J.M. 1968. 'Épica oral y épica castellana: Tradición creadora y tradición repetitiva.' *Romanische Forschungen* 80.1: 13–43.

Alonso, Dámaso. 1954. *La primitiva épica francesa a la luz de una nota emilianense.* Madrid: Consejo Superior de Investigaciones Científicas.

Alfonso-Pinto, Fátima, ed. 1999. *Las Mocedades de Rodrigo.* In Bailey, ed., 183–216.

Armistead, Samuel G. 2000. *La tradición épica de las* Mocedades de Rodrigo. Salamanca: UP.

Bailey, Matthew. 1993. *The* Poema del Cid *and the* Poema de Fernán González: *The Transformation of an Epic Tradition.* Madison, WI: Hispanic Seminary of Medieval Studies.

– 1996. 'Las últimas hazañas del conde Fernán González en la *Estoria de España*: la contribución Alfonsí.' *La corónica* 24.2: 31–40.

– ed. 1999. Las Mocedades de Rodrigo: *estudios críticos, manuscrito y edición.* King's College London Medieval Studies, XV. London: King's College London Centre for Late Antique and Medieval Studies.

– 1999a. 'Los vestigios del *Cantar de Fernán González* en las *Mocedades de Rodrigo*.' In Bailey, ed., 89–97.

– 1999b. 'Las asonancias inusitadas de las *Mocedades de Rodrigo*.' *Revista de poética medieval* 3: 9–30.

– 2003. 'Oral Composition in the Medieval Spanish Epic.' *PMLA* 118.2: 254–69.

– 2006. 'A Case for Oral Composition in the *Mester de clerecía*.' *Romance Quarterly* 53.2: 82–91.

– ed. and trans. 2007. *Las Mocedades de Rodrigo / The Youthful Deeds of Rodrigo, the Cid.* Toronto: UP and Medieval Academy of America.

Bakhtin, Mikhail Mikhailovich. 1981. *The Dialogic Imagination.* Ed. Michael Holquist. Trans. Caryl Emerson and Michael Holquist. Austin and London: Texas UP.

Bakker, Egbert. 1997. *Poetry in Speech: Orality and Homeric Discourse*. Ithaca, NY: Cornell UP.

– 1999. 'How Oral Is Oral Composition?' *Signs of Orality*. Ed. E. Anne Mackay. Leiden: Brill. 29–48.

Barton, Simon, and Richard Fletcher, ed. and trans. 2000. *The World of El Cid. Chronicles of the Spanish Reconquest*. Manchester: UP.

Bayo, Juan Carlos. 2001. 'Poetic Discourse Patterning in the *Cantar de Mio Cid*.' *Modern Language Review* 96.1: 82–91.

– 2005. 'On the Nature of the *Cantar de Mio Cid* and Its Place in Hispanic Medieval Epic.' *La corónica* 33.2: 13–27.

Burke, James F. 1973. 'The Four "Comings" of Christ in Gonzalo de Berceo's *Vida de Santa Oria*.' *Speculum* 48.2: 293–312.

Cañas, Jesús, ed. 1988. *Libro de Alexandre*. Madrid: Cátedra.

Carruthers, Mary. 1990. *The Book of Memory: A Study of Memory in Medieval Culture*. Cambridge: UP.

– 1998. *The Craft of Thought*. Cambridge: UP.

Carruthers, Mary, and Jan M. Ziolkowski, eds. 2002. *The Medieval Craft of Memory*. Philadelphia: Pennsylvania UP.

Catalán, Diego. 2001. *La épica española. Nueva documentación y nueva evaluación*. Madrid: Universidad Complutense.

Chafe, Wallace L., ed. 1980. *The Pear Stories. Cognitive, Cultural, and Linguistic Aspects of Narrative Production*. Norwood: Ablex.

– 1980. 'The Deployment of Consciousness in the Production of Narrative.' In Chafe, ed., 9–50.

– 1994. *Discourse, Consciousness, and Time*. Chicago: UP.

– 1996. 'How Consciousness Shapes Language.' *Pragmatics and Cognition* 4.1: 35–54.

Chafe, Wallace, and Jane Danielwicz. 1987. *Properties of Spoken and Written Language*. Berkeley: U of California P.

Clanchy, M.T. 1979. *From Memory to Written Record: England 1066–1307*. Cambridge: Harvard UP.

Cooper, Louis, ed. 1960. *El Liber regum. Estudio lingüístico*. Zaragoza: Instituto Fernando el Católico.

Crónica abreviada. Juan Manuel. 1958. Ed. Raymond L. Grismer and Mildred B. Grismer. Minneapolis: Burgess.

Crónica de veinte reyes. 1991. Ed. César Hernández Alonso, Enrique del Diego Simón, and Jesús María Jabato Saro. Transcription of chronicle text by José Manuel Ruiz Asencio and Mauricio Herrero Jiménez. Burgos: Ayuntamiento.

Deyermond, Alan. 1965. 'The Singer of Tales and the Mediaeval Spanish Epic.' *Bulletin of Hispanic Studies* 42: 1–8.

– 1969. *Epic Poetry and the Clergy: Studies on the* Mocedades de Rodrigo. London: Tamesis.

– 1973. 'Structural and Stylistic Patterns in the *Cantar de Mio Cid*.' *Medieval Studies in Honor of Robert White Linker by His Colleagues and Friends*. Ed. Brian Dutton et al. Valencia: Castalia. 55–71.

– 1987. *El* Cantar de Mio Cid *y la épica medieval española*. Barcelona: Sirmio.

– 1995. *La literatura perdida de la Edad Media. Catálogo y estudio, I: Épica y romances*. Salamanca: Ediciones Universidad.

– 1999. 'La autoría de las *Mocedades de Rodrigo*: un replanteamiento.' In Bailey, ed., 1–15.

Díaz-Mas, Paloma, and Carlos Mota, eds. 1998. *Proverbios morales* by Sem Tob de Carrión. Madrid: Cátedra.

Duggan, Joseph J. 1974. 'Formulaic Diction in the *Cantar de mio Cid* and the Old French Epic.' *Forum for Modern Language Studies* 10: 260–9.

– 1989a. *The 'Cantar de mio Cid': Poetic Creation in Its Economic and Social Contexts*. Cambridge: UP.

– 1989b. 'Performance and Transmission, Aural and Ocular Reception in the Twelfth- and Thirteenth-Century Vernacular Literature of France.' *Romance Philology* 43.1: 49–58.

– 2005. 'The Interface between Oral and Written Transmission of the *Cantar de Mio Cid*.' *La corónica* 33.2: 51–63.

– 2006. 'Beyond the Oxford Text: The Songs of Roland.' Ed. William W. Kibler and Leslie Zarker Morgan. *Approaches to Teaching the* Song of Roland. New York: MLA. 66–72.

Dutton, Brian. 1967. *La 'Vida de San Millán de la Cogolla' de Gonzalo de Berceo. Estudio y edición crítica*. London: Támesis.

– 1973. 'French Influences in the Spanish *Mester de Clerecía*.' Ed. Brian Dutton, J. Woodrow Hassell, Jr, and John E. Keller. *Medieval Studies in Honor of Robert White Linker by His Colleagues and Friends*. Valencia: Castalia. 73–93.

Dyer, Nancy Joe. 1979–80. '*Crónica de veinte reyes'* Use of the Cid Epic: Perspectives, Method and Rationale.' *Romance Philology* 33: 534–44.

Estévez Sola, Juan A. 1995. *Chronica Naierensis*. Turnhout: Brepols.

Falque, Emma, ed. 1990. *Historia Roderici*. In Falque, Gil, and Maya, eds, 47–98.

– ed. 2003. *Lucae Tudensis Chronicon mundi*. Turnhout: Brepols.

Falque, Emma, Juan Gil, and Antonio Maya, eds. 1990. *Chronica Hispana Saeculi XII, Pars 1* (Corpvs Christianorvm, Continuatio Mediaeualis, LXXI). Turnhout: Brepols.

Fernández González, Etelvina. 1987. 'Santo Martino de León, viajero culto y peregrino piadoso.' *Anuario de Estudios Medievales* 17: 49–65.

Fernández Ordóñez, Inés, ed. 1992. *Versión Crítica de la Estoria de España.* Madrid: Seminario Menéndez Pidal, Universidad Complutense.

– 1999. 'El taller historiográfico alfonsí. La *Estoria de España* y la *General estoria* en el marco de las obras promovidas por Alfonso el Sabio.' *El scriptorium alfonsí: de los libros de astrología a las* Cantigas de Santa María. Madrid: Editorial Complutense. 105–26.

Fernández Valverde, Juan, ed. 1987. *Roderici Ximenii de Rada, Historia de rebus Hispanie sive Historia Gothica.* Turnhout: Brepols.

Finnegan, Ruth. 1977. *Oral Poetry: Its Nature, Significance, and Social Contexts.* Cambridge: UP.

Fleischman, Suzanne. 1990a. 'Philology, Linguistics, and the Discourse of the Medieval Text.' *Speculum* 60.1: 19–37.

– 1990b. *Tense and Narrativity: From Medieval Performance to Modern Fiction.* Austin: Texas UP.

Fletcher, Richard. 1989. *The Quest for El Cid.* New York: Oxford UP.

Foley, John Miles. 1999. *Homer's Traditional Art.* University Park: Pennsylvania State UP.

Fradejas Lebrero, José. 1991. 'Valores literarios de la *Crónica de veinte reyes.*' *Crónica de veinte reyes.* Burgos: Ayuntamiento. 31–51.

Funes, Leonardo, with Felipe Tenenbaum, eds. 2004. Mocedades de Rodrigo: *Estudio y edición de los tres estados del texto.* Woodbridge, UK: Tamesis.

Geary, John Steven. 1980. *Formulaic Diction in the* Poema de Fernán González *and the* Mocedades de Rodrigo: *A Computer-Aided Analysis.* Madrid: Porrúa.

Gil, Juan. 1990. *Carmen Campidoctoris.* In Falque, Gil, and Maya, eds, 99–108. Turnholt: Brepols.

Gómez Redondo, Fernando. 1996. *Poesía española, 1, Edad Media: juglaría, clerecía y romancero.* Barcelona: Crítica.

– 1999. 'Recitación y recepción del *Cantar*: la transmisión de los modelos ideológicos.' *El Cid: de la materia épica a las crónicas caballerescas.* Ed. Carlos Alvar, Fernando Gómez Redondo, and Georges Martin. Alcalá de Henares: UP. 181–210.

Gornall, John. 1987. 'How Many Times Was the Count of Barcelona Offered His Freedom? Double Narration in the *Poema de Mio Cid.*' *Medium Aevum* 56: 65–77.

– 1996. 'Two More Cases of Double Narration in the *Cantar de mio Cid.*' *La corónica* 25.1: 85–92.

– 2005. '"A New Scene or Complimentary Treatment of the First?' A Checklist of Masked Double Narrations in the *Poema de Mio Cid.*' *Historicist Essays on*

Hispano-Medieval Narrative: In Memory of Roger M. Walker. Ed. Barry Taylor, Geoffrey West, and David G. Pattison. London: Modern Humanities Research Association. 102–14.

Harvey, L.P. 1963. 'The Metrical Irregularity of the *Cantar de Mio Cid.*' *Bulletin of Hispanic Studies* 40: 137–43.

Historia Silense. Edición crítica e introducción. 1959. Ed. Justo Pérez de Urbel y Atilano González Ruiz-Zorrilla. Madrid: Consejo Superior de Investigaciones Científicas.

Hook, David, and Antonia Long. 1999. 'Reflexiones sobre la estructura de las *Mocedades de Rodrigo.*' In Bailey, ed., 53-67.

Lacarra, María Jesús, ed. 1980. *Disciplina clericalis* by Petrus Alfonsi. Traducción de Esperanza Ducay. Zaragoza: Guara.

Lappin, Anthony. 2000. *Berceo's* Vida de Santa Oria. *Text, Translation and Commentary*. Oxford: Legenda.

Linehan, Peter. 2002. 'Fechas y sospechas sobre Lucas de Tuy.' *Anuario de estudios medivales* 32.1: 19–38.

López Guil, Itzíar, ed. 2001. *Libro de Fernán González*. Madrid: Consejo Superior de Investigaciones Científicas.

Lord, Albert Bates. 1948. 'Homer, Parry, and Huso.' *American Journal of Archaeology* 52: 34–44.

– 1960. *The Singer of Tales*. 2nd ed. Ed. Stephen Mitchell and Gregory Nagy. Cambridge: Harvard UP, 2000.

– 1995. *The Singer Resumes His Tale*. Ed. Mary Louise Lord. Ithaca, NY: Cornell UP.

Maddox, Donald, and Sara Sturm-Maddox, eds. 2002. *The Medieval French Alexander*. Albany: State U of NY P.

Martin, Georges. 1992. *Les juges de Castile: mentalités et discours historique dans l'Espagne médiévale*. Paris: Séminaire d'Études Médiévales Hispaniques, Université de Paris-XIII.

Menéndez Pidal, Gonzalo. 1951. 'Cómo trabajaron las escuelas Alfonsíes.' *Nueva Revista de Filología Hispánica* 5: 363–80.

Menéndez Pidal, Ramón, ed. 1906. *Primera crónica general*. Madrid: Bailly-Baillière e hijos. 2nd ed. Madrid: Gredos, 1955.

– ed. 1908. *Cantar de mio Cid: texto, gramática y vocabulario*. Vol. 1 (3 vols). Madrid: Bailly-Baillière e hijos.

– 1924. *Poesía juglaresca y juglares*. Madrid: Centro de Estudios Históricos.

– 1945. *Poesía juglaresca y juglares: aspectos de la historia literaria y cultural de España*. 2nd ed. Buenos Aires: Espasa-Calpe.

– 1951. *De primitiva lírica española y antigua épica*. Buenos Aires: Espasa-Calpe.

– 1963. *En torno al* Poema de mio Cid. Barcelona: EDHASA.

– 1965–6. 'Los cantores yugoeslavos y los occidentales: el *Mío Cid* y dos refundidores primitivos.' *Boletín de la Real Academia de Buenas Letras de Barcelona* 36: 195–225.

Michael, Ian, ed. 1980. *Poema de Mio Cid*. Madrid: Castalia.

– 1992. 'Orígnenes de la epopeya en España: reflexiones sobre las últimas teorías.' *Actas: II Congreso Internacional de la Asociaición Hispánica de Literatura Medieval [Segovia, del 5 al 19 de octubre de 1987].* Alcalá de Henares: UP. 71–83.

Miletich, John S. 1976–7. 'The Quest for the "Formula": A Comparative Reappraisal.' *Modern Philology* 74: 111–23.

– 1981. 'Repetition and Aesthetic Function in the *Poema de mio Cid* and South-Slavic Oral and Literary Epic.' *Bulletin of Hispanic Studies* 58: 189–96.

– 1986. 'Oral Aesthetics and Written Aesthetics: The South Slavic Case and the *Poema de Mio Cid*.' *Hispanic Studies in Honor of Alan D. Deyermond: A North American Tribute*. Ed. John S. Militech. Madison: Hispanic Seminary of Medieval Studies. 183–204.

Montaner, Alberto, ed. 1993. *Cantar de mio Cid*. Barcelona: Crítica.

– 2005. 'Revisión textual del *Cantar de mio Cid*.' *La corónica* 33.2: 137–93.

– ed. 2007. *Cantar de mio Cid*. Barcelona: Galaxia Gutenberg.

Montaner, Alberto, and Ángel Escobar. 2001. *Carmen Campidoctoris O poema latino del Campeador*. Madrid: España Nuevo Milenio.

Montgomery, Thomas. 1977. 'Oral Art in Transition.' Mio Cid *Studies*. Ed. A.D. Deyermond. London: Tamesis. 91–112.

– 1983. 'Some Singular Passages in the *Mocedades de Rodrigo*.' *Journal of Hispanic Philology* 7: 121–34.

– 1984a. 'The Lengthened Lines of the *Mocedades de Rodrigo*.' *Romance Philology* 38.1: 1–14.

– 1984b. 'Las *Mocedades de Rodrigo* y los romances.' *Josep María Solà-Solé: Homage, Homenaje, Homenatge (Miscelánea de estudios de amigos y discípulos)*. Vol II. Ed. Antonio Torres-Alcalá. Barcelona: Puvill. 119–33.

– 1993. 'Adjective Patterning in Spanish Epic.' *Olifant* 17: 168–76.

– 1998. *Medieval Spanish Epic: Mythic Roots and Ritual Language*. University Park: Penn State UP.

– 1999. 'Las *Mocedades de Rodrigo* y el *Táin Bó Cúailnge*.' In Bailey, ed., 37–52.

Parry, Adam, ed. 1971. *The Making of Homeric Verse: The Collected Papers of Milman Parry*. Oxford: Clarendon Press.

Parry, Milman. 1930. 'Studies in the Epic Technique of Oral Verse-Making.' *Harvard Studies in Classical Philology* 41: 73–147.

Pawley, Andrew, and Frances Hodgetts Syder. 1983. 'Two Puzzles for Linguistic Theory: Nativelike Selection and Nativelike Fluency.' *Language and Communication.* Ed. Jack C. Richards and Richard W. Schmidt. London: Longman. 191–225.

Pellen, René. 1998. 'Forum on Manuscript Culture in Medieval Spain.' *La corónica* 27.1: 183–205.

Poema de Santa Oria. 1928. Gonzalo de Berceo. *Cuatro poemas de Berceo.* Ed. C. Carroll Marden. Madrid: Hernando.

Powell, Brian. 1983. *Epic and Chronicle: The* Poema de Mio Cid *and the* Crónica de veinte reyes. London: Modern Humanities Research Association.

Rico, Francisco. 1985. 'La clerecía del mester.' *Hispanic Review* 53: 1–23 and 127–50.

Rubin, David C. 1995. *Memory in Oral Traditions: The Cognitive Psychology of Epic, Ballads, and Counting-out Rhymes.* New York: Oxford UP.

Russell, P.E. 1958. 'San Pedro de Cardeña and the Heroic History of the Cid.' *Medium Aevum* 28.2: 57–79.

Rychner, Jean. 1955. *La chanson de geste. Essai sur l'art épique del jongleurs.* Geneve and Lille: Société de Publications Romanes et Françaises.

Salvador Martínez, H. 1975. *El* Poema de Almería *y la épica románica.* Madrid: Gredos.

– ed. 1991. *Poema de Fernán González.* Madrid: Espasa-Calpe.

Smith, Colin. 1983. *The Making of the* Poema de mio Cid. Cambridge: UP.

– 1984. 'On the "Lost Literature" of Medieval Spain.' Guillaume d'Orange *and the Chanson de geste.* Ed. Wolfgang van Emden and Phillip E. Bennett. Reading: Société Rencesvals. 137–50.

– 1994. 'Toward a Reconciliation of Ideas about Medieval Spanish Epic.' *Modern Language Review* 89.3: 622–34.

Solalinde, A.G. 1915. 'Intervención de Alfonso X en la redacción de sus obras.' *Revista de Filología Española* 2: 283–8.

Stock, Brian. 1983. *The Implications of Literacy: Written Language and Modes of Interpretation in the Eleventh and Twelfth Centuries.* Princeton: UP.

– 1990. *Listening for the Text.* Philadelphia: Pennsylvania UP.

Tolan, John. 1993. *Petrus Alfonsi and His Medieval Readers.* Gainesville: Florida UP.

Uría, Isabel. 1997. 'Estudio preliminar.' *Milagros de Nuestra Señora* by Gonzalo de Berceo. Ed. Fernando Baños. Barcelona: Crítica. ix–xxvi.

– 2000. *Panorama crítico del* mester de clerecía. Madrid: Castalia.

Vaquero, Mercedes. 1994. 'Spanish Epic of Revolt.' *Epic and Epoch: Essays on the Interpretation and History of a Genre.* Ed. Steven M. Oberhelman et al. Lubbock: Texas Tech UP. 146–63.

– 1999. 'Las *Mocedades* en el marco de la épica.' In Bailey, ed., 99–136.

Viñayo, Antonio, ed. 1984. *Santo Martino de León. Vida y obras narradas por el Tudense.* León: Isidoriana Editorial.

Walsh, John K. 1972. 'A Possible Source for Berceo's *Vida de Santa Oria*.' *MLN* 87.2: 300–7.

Webber, Ruth House. 1980. 'Formulaic Language in the *Mocedades de Rodrigo*.' *Hispanic Review* 48: 195–211.

Wray, Alison. 2002. *Formulaic Language and the Lexicon*. Cambridge: UP.

Yarza Luaces, Joaquín. 1993–4. 'Del alfaquí sabio a los seudo-obispos: una particularidad iconográfica gótica.' *Sharq Al-Andalus* 10–11: 749–76.

Zaderenko, Irene. 1998. *Problemas de autoría, de estructura y de fuentes en el Poema de mio Cid*. Alcalá de Henares: UP.

Zumthor, Paul. 1989. *La letra y la voz. De la 'literatura' medieval*. Trans. Julián Presa. Madrid: Cátedra. Original publication, 1987. *La lettre et la voix. De la 'litterature' médiévale*. Paris: Éditions du Seuil.

– 1990. *Oral Poetry: An Introduction*. Trans. Kathryn Murphy-Judy. Foreword by Walter J. Ong. Minneapolis: UP. Original publication, 1983. *Introduction à la poésie orale*. Paris: Éditions du Seuil.

Index